The 24-Hour War Story with ChatGPT

Andrew Parry

Published by Andrew Parry, 2025.

THE 24-HOUR WAR STORY WITH CHATGPT

First edition. April 23, 2025.

ISBN: 979-8231975624

Written by Andrew Parry.

Table of Contents

What Makes War Drama So Powerful

There's something about war dramas that never fails to grip audiences. Whether it's a novel, a short story, or a screenplay, stories set during wartime carry an emotional weight that hits us deep. Maybe it's the constant life-or-death stakes, or maybe it's how war strips characters down to their rawest, most vulnerable selves. Either way, there's no denying that war drama has the potential to leave a lasting impact on the reader or viewer. The genre holds up a mirror to humanity—sometimes reflecting our greatest courage, and other times, our darkest impulses. What makes war drama so powerful is that it takes everything we understand about conflict and amplifies it with a backdrop of chaos, urgency, and emotional intensity.

War drama is one of the few genres where the stakes are already naturally high. You're not inventing a situation where the characters might lose something minor; you're placing them in a world where their very survival is at risk every moment. And because death and danger are such constant companions in these stories, every small victory, every act of kindness, every flicker of hope shines even brighter. Audiences don't just observe—they feel. They root for the hero not just because they're brave, but because they're hanging by a thread in a world unraveling around them. That rawness, that desperation, that impossible resilience—those are the things that make war drama unforgettable.

What really gives war drama its power, though, is its ability to explore big themes through personal stories. You could write about a huge battle or a famous campaign, but what grips people are the individuals caught in the middle of it. Their fears, their beliefs, their sacrifices, and their small moments of humanity are what make the story matter. War drama isn't just about bullets flying and bombs dropping. It's about the soldier who carries a photo of his family, the medic who can't save everyone, the child who doesn't understand why her village is burning, the lover who waits but never hears back. These characters anchor the sweeping scale of war into something real and deeply relatable.

War drama also makes it easy to examine the best and worst of human nature. Characters are put in extreme situations, and in those moments, we get to see what they're really made of. Some become heroes. Some break. Some betray everything they once believed in. Others find purpose in the ashes. This kind of emotional transformation is perfect for storytelling. And as a writer, you can push your characters further in a war drama than almost any other genre because you have that constant pressure cooker of danger and urgency working in your favor.

There's also a natural structure that war drama often falls into, which makes it easier to outline your plot. Most wars have a beginning, a middle, and an end. They have major turning points, climaxes, and resolutions. You can use that structure to shape your narrative, creating tension and release, buildup and payoff. It allows you to blend historical or fictional events with strong character arcs. Whether you're working with real conflicts like World War II or entirely fictional ones in a fantasy world, the war provides a built-in frame for your drama.

Another thing that makes war drama so compelling is the moral complexity. Few genres allow you to play in such gray areas. In war, good and evil aren't always clear-cut. Sometimes good people do terrible things to survive. Sometimes enemies turn out to be just as human as the protagonists. This complexity is a goldmine for writers. It lets you challenge your audience, force them to wrestle with difficult questions, and show how fragile morality becomes when pushed to the edge. War drama gives you the freedom to explore those moments where right and wrong blur together, and where choices aren't easy.

There's also the timelessness of war drama. It doesn't matter whether you're writing about ancient Sparta, the trenches of World War I, or a future intergalactic battle. The emotions stay the same. Fear, loyalty, grief, courage, love—these are universal experiences. They resonate across generations. That means your story, no matter what time or place it's set in, can feel urgent and relevant to modern readers. People are drawn to these stories because they reveal truths about humanity that are just as real today as they were a hundred or a thousand years ago.

War dramas are also incredibly visual, which makes them great candidates for screenplays and films. You have the backdrop of epic battles, ruined cities, crowded refugee camps, and tense military headquarters. You can create visuals that are both grand and intimate. A line of soldiers marching into fog. A lone survivor crawling through the mud. A family clutching each other in a bomb shelter. These images stay with people. And when you combine those visuals with emotionally charged scenes, you create something unforgettable.

Then there's the catharsis. Audiences come to war dramas knowing they're going to be taken through the wringer. They expect heartbreak. They brace for loss. But they also crave that one moment of hope, that one act of redemption, that single, flickering light in the darkness. A good war drama leaves people breathless and broken—and still wanting more. It reminds us how precious life is, how strong the human spirit can be, and how love and honor can survive even the worst hell imaginable.

Using ChatGPT to write a war drama allows you to dive straight into the deep end. You can brainstorm the story in real time, ask for character sketches, test dialogue, and build scenes with emotional weight. You don't have to wait for inspiration—you can feed the AI a premise or an emotional beat and see what comes out. And that speed is perfect for a genre like this, where you need to capture urgency, momentum, and human intensity without getting bogged down in the planning phase. The AI can help you stay in the flow and push your story forward quickly.

So when we talk about what makes war drama powerful, we're really talking about a blend of high stakes, emotional vulnerability, moral complexity, and timeless themes. It's about putting ordinary people in extraordinary situations and seeing what happens. It's about showing both the horror and the heroism that war brings out. And more than anything, it's about telling stories that feel urgent, relevant, and deeply human. If you can tap into that—if you can find that beating heart inside the chaos—then you've already won half the battle as a writer.

War drama is one of the most emotionally resonant genres you can explore, and with the help of ChatGPT, you can bring those stories to life in a way that feels immediate, gripping, and unforgettable. The battlefield is set. The characters are waiting. All that's left is to start writing.

Starting With the End in Mind

When you're writing a war drama, one of the most powerful tools you can use is to start with the end in mind. This doesn't just mean knowing how the story wraps up in terms of plot—it means understanding the emotional destination, the final note you want to leave your audience with, and the transformation your characters will go through to get there. That last image, that final feeling, that closing line—those are the things that stay with readers and viewers long after the story ends. Starting with the end gives you a kind of compass. It shows you what matters most and helps you build everything else to serve that final, unforgettable moment.

In a genre like war drama, where the stakes are already so high, the ending carries even more weight. It's not just about whether the protagonist lives or dies. It's about what they've learned, what they've lost, what they've endured. War changes people, and your ending should reflect that transformation. Maybe your hero becomes hardened and cynical. Maybe they find a new sense of purpose. Maybe they walk away from the war broken, or maybe they walk away stronger than ever. However it ends, the journey must feel earned—and the only way to make sure it's earned is to know where you're heading before you start.

Let's say you want your story to end with a soldier walking away from a battlefield, alone but alive, carrying the memory of a fallen comrade. That tells you a lot about the story already. It tells you that loss is going to be central. It tells you that there's a friendship or bond that needs to be developed. It tells you that, even if there's survival, there's going to be grief. From that single image, you can start to work backwards. You can figure out where the friendship began, what trials they went through together, what decisions led to the final outcome, and how your character grows through it all. By knowing the end, you can shape the middle with intention.

This method also helps when you're using ChatGPT to generate your content. If you can feed the AI a specific ending you're working toward, it can help you brainstorm scenes that logically build up to it. You might say, "I want a story that ends with a nurse in a field hospital losing her last patient and questioning her faith in humanity," and suddenly, ChatGPT can help you map out a sequence of events that brings her to that moment. It gives your writing a direction and your brainstorming a focus. You're not wandering blindly—you're marching toward something.

Another benefit of starting with the end is that it keeps your themes grounded. If your ending is about redemption, then you'll want to weave in situations where your characters are tempted, broken, or morally challenged. If your ending is about futility, you might want to build up hope early on, only to crush it by the final act. War dramas often wrestle with massive themes—honor, sacrifice, brotherhood, disillusionment, survival. These themes feel more powerful when they arc clearly toward a definitive ending. When you know how the story will close, you can set up contrasts and echoes that make that closure hit even harder.

The end also shapes the tone of your entire story. A hopeful ending might suggest more uplifting or poetic moments throughout, even if tragedy is present. A bleak ending might push you to create darker, more intense scenes. A bittersweet ending will likely mean balancing both. When you begin with that final note in mind, you can tune the rest of your narrative to hit the right emotional frequency. You can decide when to pull back, when to lean in, and when to let a scene linger, because you already know the emotional payoff you're working toward.

Let's look at a few examples. Think about *Saving Private Ryan*. The whole film is constructed to deliver on that final moment in the cemetery, where the elderly Ryan asks if he was a good man, if he earned the life others gave their lives to preserve. That question—the need for meaning, the weight of survival—is baked into every decision made in the story.

You feel the arc building toward that moment because the filmmakers started with the emotional impact they wanted the audience to feel and then designed everything else around it. It's not just about the plot. It's about the purpose.

Or take *The Pianist*. The final scene, where Szpilman is once again playing piano on the radio after surviving so much devastation, offers a haunting mix of beauty and emptiness. You know from the beginning that the story is about survival through art, about the resilience of the human spirit in the face of atrocity. That ending only works because everything else has been leading us there—from the first bombed note to the last lonely key.

Even in fictional or speculative war dramas, this technique applies. If your story ends with a young fighter in a futuristic war realizing that both sides were manipulated by unseen powers, then the path you write will explore themes of illusion, control, and the search for truth. Each twist in the plot becomes more meaningful because you've already chosen the destination. That final revelation has been baked into every scene leading up to it.

When you write with the end in mind, it becomes easier to avoid filler. Every scene has a purpose. Every character relationship contributes to the resolution. You're not just writing to see what happens—you're writing because you already know what must happen, and you're layering the journey with meaning and foreshadowing. This helps keep your pacing tight and your narrative clean, especially when you're using AI to assist you. ChatGPT can be a fantastic tool, but it works best when you guide it with clarity. Give it the end, and it will help you write the beginning and the middle with confidence.

Of course, starting with the end doesn't mean you can't change your mind. Sometimes the story evolves in unexpected ways. A character becomes more compelling than you anticipated. A subplot takes on new life. That's fine. But even then, having a starting point—a planned ending—gives you something to push against. You can always adapt as you go. The goal is to avoid writing aimlessly. War dramas don't work if they meander. They need structure. They need drive. And nothing gives a story drive quite like a destination.

So, before you type that first line, close your eyes and imagine the final scene. Picture the battlefield after the dust has settled. Picture who's still standing and who's not. Picture the look on your protagonist's face. Are they relieved? Hollow? Changed? Picture the final words spoken, the final thoughts that echo. That's your anchor. That's the moment everything else builds toward.

Write that ending down. Describe it in a few sentences. And then let ChatGPT help you build the road that leads there. The more vividly you can see the end, the more powerfully you can tell the journey—and the more unforgettable your war drama will become.

Finding Your Big War Idea

Writing a war drama starts with one thing above all else—an idea strong enough to carry the emotional and narrative weight of an entire story. This isn't just any idea. It's your *big war idea*, the core concept that will shape everything from your setting and characters to the themes and pacing. It has to be something that fires you up, something that makes you want to tell the story so badly that you can't shake it. A good war drama doesn't come from just knowing about battles and strategies—it comes from an emotional connection to the story you want to tell, and that story begins with a powerful, central concept.

So where do you find this big idea? The trick is not to start with the war itself. Start with people. Start with human emotion. Ask yourself what this story is really about beneath the gunfire and explosions. Maybe it's about a father trying to get back to his child. Maybe it's about a soldier who deserts and pretends to be someone else. Maybe it's about a war photographer who stops taking pictures and starts saving lives. When you peel back the surface, the war becomes the backdrop—and your big idea becomes the engine that drives the story forward.

You can get inspiration from history, but you don't have to stay chained to it. Some of the best war dramas mix fact with fiction, blending real events with personal invention. You might find your idea in a single sentence from a history book or a passing mention of a minor figure in a documentary. You might stumble across a letter, a diary, a quote, a photograph—and boom, a whole world opens up. ChatGPT is a great tool for this stage. Just type something like "Give me unique war drama ideas based on lesser-known WWII events" and see what comes back. Use the AI as a springboard to help you spark fresh, untold perspectives.

Think about scale, too. Is your story going to be massive in scope, following an entire battalion through years of combat? Or is it small and intimate, focusing on one character's internal war during a single night? There's no wrong answer. But you need to know which kind of story you want to tell. Your big idea has to feel big to *you*, even if it's about just one person. Don't underestimate the power of a quiet moment in a loud world. Sometimes a single soldier saving a child from a collapsing building can be more powerful than an entire battlefield of screaming chaos. The intimacy is what hooks the reader and grounds the emotion.

You also need to know why this story matters. Not in a preachy or moralistic way—but on a personal level. Why this war? Why this moment? Why this character? What is it about this situation that calls out to you as a storyteller? The more personal the connection, the more emotional truth you'll bring to the page. And the more emotional truth you bring, the more your audience will care. War dramas that feel hollow usually start from a place of spectacle. The ones that hit hard start from a place of heart.

Themes help shape your idea into something deeper. Let's say you want to tell a story about a woman who disguises herself as a man to fight in the American Civil War. That's a solid premise, but what's the theme? Is it about identity? Is it about sacrifice? Is it about breaking rules in the name of love? If you know the theme, you can explore your big idea from all angles, layering in meaning scene by scene. A theme doesn't have to be complicated. It can be something as simple as survival, redemption, or the cost of loyalty. But once you choose it, your story begins to take on shape and purpose.

Genre crossovers can also help you find your idea. What if your war drama is also a mystery? Or a romance? Or a coming-of-age story? Combining genres helps freshen things up and can make your idea stand out. You might write about a detective trying to solve a murder in a war-torn city. Or a soldier who falls in love with the enemy. Or a teenager who becomes a reluctant freedom fighter after losing his family. These combinations give your war drama a new flavor—and they help you avoid clichés.

Sometimes the best ideas come from flipping something on its head. Take a classic war story and look at it from the opposite perspective. What if the "enemy" isn't the enemy at all? What if the hero of your story is someone history forgot—or someone who never wanted to be remembered in the first place? Try writing about someone on the fringes of the war: a journalist, a medic, a deserter, a refugee, a child, a spy who never sees the battlefield. These characters offer fresh entry points into old settings. And when you bring something new to a genre as well-trodden as war drama, you stand out.

If you ever feel stuck, lean into ChatGPT. You can ask it for five war drama storylines involving betrayal, or three emotional arcs about post-war redemption, or ten potential protagonists for a Korean War setting. You can feed it your half-baked concept and ask for ways to expand or twist it. Don't just use it to generate ideas—use it to *shape* them. Treat the AI like a creative writing partner, someone who's always ready to brainstorm with you, and push back if the ideas feel generic until you find one that clicks emotionally.

Your big war idea should always be something you can sum up in a sentence. Not because you're trying to pitch it right away, but because clarity matters. If you can't say what your story is about in one breath, you might not be clear enough on the core of it yet. That sentence becomes your guidepost. It helps you stay on track when the story starts to sprawl. Something like, "A wounded German soldier hides in a French village where the resistance shelters him, forcing him to question everything he's ever believed," tells you a lot. You've got the setting, the character, the conflict, and a deep emotional core all in one line.

Once you've got your idea, write it down and sit with it for a while. Let it grow. Ask questions. Test it. Why this war? Why this character? Why now? What does the character want? What stands in their way? What's at stake if they fail? The more you interrogate the idea, the stronger your story becomes. And when you feel ready to begin writing, you won't be fumbling for direction—you'll already be halfway there.

The power of a war drama lies in its humanity. The right idea can carry that weight, reach across cultures and time periods, and speak to the universal truth that war changes everything. It's not about glorifying violence or celebrating destruction. It's about using the backdrop of war to explore resilience, love, grief, identity, and what it means to be human when everything is falling apart.

So dig deep. Find the idea that stirs something in you. Then let that idea lead you into the trenches, the foxholes, the shelters, the skies, or the ruins—and tell the story only you can tell.

Choosing the Right Conflict

Every war drama begins with conflict—but not just any conflict. Choosing the right conflict is what gives your story its soul. It's what defines the world your characters are living in and the conditions that push them to grow, change, or break. The conflict you choose becomes the stage where your themes will unfold and your emotional beats will land. Whether it's a global war, a civil war, a fictional conflict in a fantasy world, or a quiet psychological war inside a single mind, the type of conflict you choose sets the tone for everything else.

The most obvious kind of conflict in war drama is external and large-scale. Think about World War I or II, the Vietnam War, the Korean War, the Gulf War, or even imagined future wars in a sci-fi setting. These wars come with instantly recognizable stakes—death, survival, the collapse of nations—and built-in drama that helps carry your narrative. But even in these big wars, the best stories focus on the personal. The battlefield might be huge, but your story lives and dies on the human level. So when you're choosing the conflict, don't just think about which war to set it in—think about how that war interacts with the inner life of your characters.

You could also choose a smaller, more focused type of war. Civil wars, revolutions, resistance movements, occupations, and insurgencies all offer different dynamics. A resistance story during a brutal occupation might center on a community rather than a traditional army. That opens up room for characters like teachers, farmers, or children to become unexpected heroes. These types of conflicts also often carry deeper emotional tension because the enemy is closer—sometimes even a neighbor, a family member, or someone once trusted. The emotional stakes rise sharply when the lines between friend and foe are blurred.

And then there's the choice of fictional conflicts. Maybe you're creating your own imagined war for a future or alternate-history setting. This gives you complete control over the causes, sides, and consequences, but it also requires you to be precise in how you construct the world. Even if it's fictional, the war still needs to feel real. People still need to bleed. Choices still need to hurt. With a made-up war, your challenge becomes grounding it in recognizable human emotion. This is where ChatGPT can be helpful—ask it to help you build out the geopolitical roots, factions, and history of your fictional conflict so you don't lose the realism in the make-believe.

The kind of war you choose should reflect the themes you want to explore. If your story is about sacrifice, a massive, drawn-out war might be the best canvas. If it's about betrayal, a war of occupation where trust is fragile might be better. If it's about identity, a civil war where a character is caught between both sides can turn that theme into something painful and urgent. You don't need to spell out the theme up front—but choosing the right conflict helps the theme show up naturally in everything from setting to character decisions.

Conflict in a war drama isn't just about who's fighting whom. It's also about *why*. The political, cultural, or personal reasons behind the war should inform the way the story unfolds. Ask yourself what's at stake—not just for the world, but for your main character. Maybe the war is about oil or territory or ideology on the surface, but for your character, it's about finding purpose after loss. Or reclaiming something taken. Or running from guilt. You want to connect the larger conflict to a specific emotional journey. That's where the drama lives.

Sometimes, the best stories come from characters who are in conflict with their own side. Think about the soldier who starts to question the cause they're fighting for. Or the officer who has to choose between following orders and doing what's right. These internal conflicts add complexity and emotional depth. They make the character more than a pawn—they make them human. Choosing a war that allows for moral ambiguity and ethical dilemmas is often the key to writing something memorable.

Also consider how visible or invisible the war will be in your story. Some war dramas are set entirely on the front lines, with constant gunfire and chaos. Others barely show the battlefield at all, focusing instead on the quiet moments between battles or the lives of civilians trying to carry on. The absence of visible conflict can be just as powerful as its presence. It's about the psychological toll, the suspense, the dread that hangs over everything. Choosing a conflict where the violence is felt more than seen can create a slow-burning kind of drama that lingers in the mind.

The right conflict also determines who your protagonist will be. A trench war might naturally suggest a soldier as the lead, while an urban occupation could give you a resistance fighter, a shopkeeper, or even a child as the main character. The setting shapes who can exist within it and what kind of choices they're allowed to make. So pick a conflict that makes your character's journey possible and meaningful. Don't be afraid to think outside the usual roles. There are endless angles to explore, and war touches everyone differently.

When you're using ChatGPT to help generate or flesh out your story, be clear about the conflict you've chosen. If it's historical, specify the war, the country, and the year. Ask for character types that would logically exist in that context. If it's fictional, describe the factions, the geography, and the causes of the war. Let the AI help you brainstorm locations, emotional arcs, or even battle strategies that make the conflict feel real. A good war drama depends on the authenticity of the world—and the more you understand the nature of the conflict, the more grounded your story will be.

Sometimes it helps to write a short paragraph that summarizes the conflict before you begin. Something like, "The story takes place during the early months of the Spanish Civil War, as fascist forces close in on a small village where the local schoolteacher is forced to choose between neutrality and resistance." That simple setup gives you direction. You know where the tension is, who it's affecting, and how personal it will be. From there, everything else—character arcs, scenes, dialogue—starts to fall into place.

Remember that the war is not the story. The war is the condition. It's the pressure cooker. It's the storm outside the window while the real drama plays out inside someone's head, or home, or heart. Choosing the right conflict is about setting the right stage. The more specific and emotionally rich your conflict is, the more potential your war drama has to be something people can feel in their gut.

So take your time at this stage. Research. Brainstorm. Use ChatGPT to test different scenarios. Don't settle until the conflict feels right—not just for the plot, but for the journey you want to take your audience on. Once you've chosen the right war, you'll know it. Because the story will start whispering to you, louder than gunfire.

Picking the Right Era of War

When writing a war drama, the era you choose to set your story in changes everything. It defines not just the weapons and uniforms, but the politics, the mindset, the technology, the societal roles, and the emotional texture of the world your characters live in. Picking the right era of war is like choosing the lens through which your story will be viewed. You can tell a story about love, courage, betrayal, redemption, or survival in any timeline—but the meaning and impact of that story will shift depending on the era it plays out in. This chapter is all about helping you lock in that perfect time period for your narrative, so that everything else you build feels organically tied to that world.

Sometimes writers rush this decision, thinking that war is war, and as long as there's conflict, it doesn't really matter when it takes place. But it does matter. A World War I drama feels completely different from one set during the Vietnam War or the Syrian Civil War. Each of these eras comes with its own historical baggage, unique moral questions, and emotional undercurrents. Choosing the right era isn't about picking the one with the coolest battles or most familiar setting—it's about finding the era that best supports the story you're trying to tell.

If your war drama centers around themes like loss of innocence, futility, or the dehumanizing effects of modern warfare, then World War I might be the perfect fit. The trenches, the endless stalemates, the sense that no side really "won"—this era is tailor-made for bleak, philosophical war dramas. It's a world where the brutality is matched by a kind of numb, mechanical cruelty, and where characters can drift into despair while still clinging to slivers of humanity.

On the other hand, if your story is about moral clarity, camaraderie, and the fight between good and evil, World War II might be your ideal backdrop. It's one of the most commonly used eras in war drama for a reason. The stakes were global. The villains were unmistakable. The cost was enormous. But be careful—because this era has been covered so thoroughly, you'll need a fresh angle. Maybe it's from the perspective of a child in an occupied town, a nurse on the Eastern Front, or a spy hiding in plain sight. Use ChatGPT to brainstorm roles and perspectives you haven't seen before in this context.

The Vietnam War shifts the emotional tone once again. It's the perfect era for stories about disillusionment, confusion, moral ambiguity, and trauma. This war was televised. It was protested. It was misunderstood, and many who fought in it came home feeling abandoned or betrayed. It's an era rich with emotional complexity, making it fertile ground for psychological war dramas or stories where the enemy is not just on the battlefield but in the mind. This setting is especially powerful if your story is about a protagonist who questions everything they were taught to believe.

If you're drawn to a more recent or even ongoing conflict—like Iraq, Afghanistan, Ukraine, or Syria—then you're stepping into a world that feels modern and personal. These wars often involve advanced technology, urban combat, drones, counterinsurgency tactics, and blurred lines between soldier and civilian. The emotional terrain here is all about survival in a shifting, often confusing landscape. Characters might struggle with cultural clashes, moral uncertainty, or the difficulty of knowing who the enemy really is. This is a great fit if your war drama is about nuance, modern politics, or the personal cost of asymmetrical warfare.

Then there's the choice to go far back in time—Napoleonic wars, the Crusades, feudal Japan, ancient Greece, or Rome. These settings offer a whole new palette of storytelling. If you're drawn to epic storytelling, political intrigue, hand-to-hand combat, or stories of honor, duty, and legacy, an older war might give you the drama you're looking for. There's a kind of mythic weight to these eras. They let you work with larger-than-life characters, codes of honor, and sweeping arcs. The research might be heavier, but the payoff can be huge—especially if you're blending historical authenticity with emotional resonance.

And of course, you can invent your own era. A future war. An alternate timeline. A fantastical world inspired by history but not bound by it. When you choose a fictional era, you have total freedom—but that means you have to do more world-building work. What caused this war? What are the ideologies at play? What does the world look like? What are the consequences of winning or losing? Use ChatGPT to help you generate the politics, the culture, the technology, and even the languages if you want. A fictional war era gives you flexibility, but it also demands consistency. Every rule you create has to feel real to the characters who live in it.

One way to help decide the right era is to ask yourself this: what kind of emotional tone do I want the story to have? Is it bleak and cold? Then World War I might serve you well. Is it chaotic and paranoid? Then the Cold War or Vietnam might be your match. Is it futuristic and high-concept? Then create your own war from scratch. Is it about tradition and family legacy? Then maybe go medieval or classical. The emotional tone should match the time period, because when those two things work together, the story feels seamless.

Also, consider who your characters are and what roles they can realistically play in a given era. If you want to write about a female soldier, you're going to have more freedom in modern or futuristic settings, unless you're specifically telling a story about someone breaking the rules in an earlier era. If your protagonist is a journalist, resistance fighter, or nurse, some eras will lend themselves better than others. Your setting has to support the kind of journey your character is going to go on. And once you figure that out, the whole story starts to feel like it's clicking into place.

Use ChatGPT to test out different eras by writing short synopses for the same story set in different time periods. You might be surprised how different a story feels when it's moved from World War II to the Syrian Civil War, or from the Napoleonic era to a futuristic planetary battle. This technique helps you find the version that feels richest, the one with the most potential for emotion, theme, and character.

Ultimately, picking the right era of war isn't about what's popular or visually impressive. It's about choosing a world that allows your story to breathe. It's about creating a context that amplifies the emotions you want to explore and gives your characters the right kind of pressure to grow, fall, or transform. When you pick the right time period, the war doesn't just exist in the background—it becomes the atmosphere, the weather system, the gravity field in which everything else takes shape.

So take your time with this decision. Play with ideas. Test out scenarios. And once you find the era that resonates most, let it shape your story from the inside out. Let it guide your tone, inform your dialogue, influence your characters' choices, and steep every scene in a sense of time, place, and consequence. That's when you know you've picked the right era—and that's when your war drama will start to come alive.

What Kind of War Story Are You Telling?

Before you write a single word of your war drama, you've got to answer one deceptively simple question: what kind of war story are you telling? You might think, well, it's a story set during a war, so it's a war story—end of discussion. But that's just the surface. War drama is a wide and incredibly flexible genre, and within it are all kinds of subtypes and emotional flavors. Understanding the *kind* of war story you're telling gives you the clarity to make stronger choices about structure, pacing, tone, and character development. It's like knowing what dish you're cooking before you start grabbing ingredients.

You could be writing a survival story. This is probably one of the most common and visceral forms of war drama. These are the stories about hanging on by a thread, about dodging bullets, hiding in ruins, crawling through mud, escaping from captivity, or enduring against impossible odds. The focus is often on raw instinct, physical limits, and the will to live. Stories like *The Pianist*, *1917*, or *Come and See* are good examples. The emotional core of these tales is usually endurance—what it takes to survive, and what kind of person emerges at the other end.

Or maybe your story is a brotherhood story. These are about bonds formed in the fire of combat. Think *Band of Brothers*, *Platoon*, or *Saving Private Ryan*. The focus is on camaraderie, trust, loss, and shared trauma. If you're drawn to stories of friendship and loyalty under fire, then you're writing a brotherhood war drama. These stories work best when the relationships between the characters are as intense and layered as the battles themselves. The war becomes the crucible that forges or fractures those bonds.

You could also be writing a coming-of-age story set during war. Maybe it's about a teenage conscript forced into combat. Maybe it's about a child growing up in an occupied country. These stories are about transformation—where a character is thrown into a violent world and forced to grow up fast. *Grave of the Fireflies* and *Jojo Rabbit* are haunting examples of this kind of war drama. These stories are emotional landmines because they deal with innocence lost, the distortion of childhood, and how war shapes identity in irreversible ways.

Another path is the moral dilemma story. These are stories where the real war is inside the character. Maybe a soldier is ordered to do something they know is wrong. Maybe a commander has to choose between sacrificing a few to save many. Maybe a spy has to betray someone they care about for the greater good. These are the *gray zone* war stories. *The Deer Hunter*, *Atonement*, and *Eye in the Sky* all live here. The emotional core is guilt, conflict, or moral paralysis. These stories lean heavily on internal conflict, and they're goldmines for character-driven drama.

Then there are resistance stories. These usually center on civilian characters or underdog fighters living under occupation or fighting back in secret. Think *Defiance*, *The Wind That Shakes the Barley*, or *Inglourious Basterds*. These stories are usually about rebellion, courage in the face of oppression, or the cost of fighting for freedom. The tension often comes from hiding in plain sight, passing messages, dodging informants, and staying one step ahead of the enemy. These stories are rich in suspense and often carry themes of justice, vengeance, or hope.

You might be telling a home-front story. These don't take place on the battlefield at all but instead focus on those left behind. Spouses, parents, children, and entire communities coping with the absence or loss of loved ones, dealing with rationing, or working in factories to support the war effort. *The English Patient* and *Letters from Iwo Jima* explore this side of the genre. These stories are quieter but no less powerful. They deal with absence, fear, longing, and emotional survival. They're often incredibly intimate and character-driven.

And then there are political or ideological war dramas. These are stories that dig into the causes of war, the power plays, the decisions behind the scenes, and the way ideology turns into conflict. These stories might follow generals, politicians, or thinkers caught in the storm of war. *Thirteen Days*, *Paths of Glory*, and *The Lives of Others* are great examples. These stories are dense, thoughtful, and sometimes philosophical. They explore how ideas turn into bombs and how decisions made in high places ripple out to the lives of millions.

You might even be working on a war story that's about redemption. Maybe your protagonist did something horrible early in the war, and the entire story is about trying to make it right. Maybe they were a coward, and now they have to be brave. Maybe they lost someone and now have to protect someone else. Redemption arcs are powerful in war dramas because the stakes are so extreme and forgiveness so rare. The emotional payoff, when done right, is massive.

Of course, many war dramas don't fit neatly into just one category. You could have a survival story that's also a redemption story. A coming-of-age story that's also about brotherhood. A resistance story with strong ideological conflict woven in. That's perfectly fine. But knowing which *kind* of story is dominant helps you organize your priorities. It shapes how you handle the emotional beats and what moments get the spotlight.

Using ChatGPT, you can actually test this. Feed it your basic premise and ask: "What kind of war story is this?" or "What emotional arc fits best with this war drama concept?" You can also generate different versions of your story through each lens. For example, take your idea and ask ChatGPT to spin it as a survival story, then as a moral dilemma, then as a coming-of-age narrative. You'll quickly see which version feels the most emotionally honest to you—and that's the version you should pursue.

Once you know what kind of war story you're telling, everything else starts to fall into place. Your character arcs, your tone, your pacing, even your ending—these are all shaped by the type of story you're writing. If you're writing a brotherhood story, your key scenes will be about group dynamics, shared trauma, and sacrifice. If it's a resistance story, you'll need tension, secrecy, and clever subversion. If it's a redemption story, your focus is going to be on personal transformation.

So take a moment. Step back from the explosions and uniforms and ask yourself: What is this really about? What kind of journey is this character on? What emotional truth am I trying to reach by the end of the story? When you answer that honestly, the kind of war story you're telling will become clear—and that clarity will be your compass through the entire writing process.

Grounding Your Story in History or Imagination

Every great war drama lives in a world that feels real. Whether you're writing a historically accurate account of a specific battle or a fictional war in a completely invented universe, your story needs roots. It needs context. It needs rules that make it feel believable. So when it comes to grounding your story, you have two major paths: history or imagination. Both are valid, both are powerful, and both come with their own advantages and challenges. What matters most is that you fully commit to the one you choose—and that you build a world that's rich enough to support the emotional journey of your characters.

If you're grounding your story in real history, you've got a huge advantage right out of the gate. The world already exists. The uniforms, the dates, the battles, the politics—it's all there, waiting to be used. That doesn't mean your job is easier, but it does mean you've got a map. You can do the research, find real stories and real people, and let history inspire your narrative. There's an immediate emotional weight to a story that takes place during an actual conflict. Readers and viewers bring their own understanding, their own expectations, their own emotional connection to that era. A story set during the Holocaust, or the Vietnam War, or the Battle of Stalingrad already comes with gravity—and that can work in your favor.

But writing historical war drama also means you've got a responsibility. You have to respect the truth, even if you're fictionalizing the details. You don't have to be a historian, but you do need to understand the basic facts and avoid bending them just to fit your plot. Readers can smell inaccuracy a mile away, and nothing pulls them out of a story faster than a scene that feels lazy or off-base. The good news is, ChatGPT can help you with this. Ask for timelines, battle summaries, historical figures, political dynamics, cultural norms, even daily life in the time period. You can use AI to fact-check your scenes or generate historically grounded character sketches without getting lost in research rabbit holes.

Historical settings also give you the chance to spotlight voices that don't often get heard. Maybe your story focuses on an African regiment in World War I. Or a female spy working with the resistance in occupied France. Or a group of Indigenous soldiers sent to fight in a war they never chose. The history books often focus on the generals and the famous battles—but war touches every kind of person. Telling a story from an unexpected point of view can make even a well-known conflict feel new and emotionally gripping.

On the other hand, you might choose to ground your story in pure imagination. Maybe you're building a world that's loosely inspired by real wars but completely fictional in terms of names, places, and outcomes. Maybe you're setting your war drama in a dystopian future, a fantasy realm, or even an alternate version of Earth. That choice gives you total freedom. You're not boxed in by historical events. You can explore themes in symbolic or exaggerated ways. You can design your own uniforms, write your own battle strategies, and create your own rules for how war is fought and what it costs.

But freedom also means more responsibility to build something believable. Your invented world still needs rules. It still needs logic. Even in fantasy or science fiction settings, people need to feel that the world operates consistently, that the war has clear causes and consequences, and that the characters are shaped by the world around them. This is where a lot of writers get stuck—because the temptation is to throw in cool ideas without stitching them together into a cohesive world. ChatGPT can be your world-building partner here. Use it to help flesh out the history of your fictional nations, their ideologies, their alliances and betrayals. Ask it to describe what a futuristic battlefield might look like or how civilians might survive under a magical occupation. Keep pushing until the world feels real, even if it's unreal.

The benefit of fictional war settings is that they let you explore timeless ideas in a way that feels fresh. You can write about the trauma of combat, the loss of innocence, or the fight for freedom without being tied to specific dates or historical events. Sometimes fiction allows you to go deeper because you're not weighed down by facts. You can explore emotions in more abstract or symbolic ways. You can twist the rules of reality just enough to shed new light on familiar truths.

Some of the best war dramas fall somewhere in between. Think of stories that are *inspired* by real events but not bound by them. A war that looks like WWII but takes place in a fictional country. A revolution that mirrors real uprisings but with different names and outcomes. These hybrid stories give you the weight of historical resonance with the freedom of invention. They allow you to explore *what if* scenarios. What if the war never ended? What if the wrong side won? What if history took one small turn in the other direction? You're not rewriting history—you're exploring its emotional echoes.

So how do you decide which way to go? Ask yourself what the heart of your story is. Is it about something specific that happened in a real war? Do you want to honor real people, real places, real pain? Then go historical. Do the research. Respect the facts. Let the truth shape your fiction. Or is your story more about theme and emotion? Do you want to build a metaphor, a warning, a poetic vision of conflict? Then imagination might be your path. Build your world. Make it feel real. Use war as the furnace where your characters are forged.

If you're unsure, write a scene in both styles and see which one feels more alive. Write a scene between two characters in a WWI trench. Then write the same emotional scene in a cratered battlefield on a distant planet. See which version grabs you. Which one sparks more dialogue, more conflict, more visual detail? Sometimes the world you choose isn't the one you expected—it's the one that pulls the most emotion out of you as a writer.

Whether you're grounding your story in history or imagination, the same rule applies: make it real. Make the world feel lived in. Make the war feel consequential. Make the people feel like they're part of something they didn't ask for but have to survive anyway. Because war—real or imagined—is never just about nations clashing. It's about people caught in the gears. It's about life interrupted. And whether your story lives in the past, the future, or somewhere entirely fictional, your job is to make that world feel urgent, alive, and painfully human.

Crafting a Powerful Central Character

A war drama lives and dies on the strength of its central character. It doesn't matter how explosive the battles are or how historically accurate the setting is—if your protagonist isn't compelling, the story won't stick. What makes a war story unforgettable is not the war itself but how the war transforms the person at the center of it. That's your job as the writer: to craft a character who doesn't just survive the war, but changes because of it. Who they are at the beginning needs to be fundamentally different from who they are at the end, even if they don't make it to the end at all.

The first step is deciding what kind of transformation your character is going to undergo. War puts enormous pressure on people, and pressure reveals character. Is your protagonist someone who begins idealistic and slowly becomes hardened? Someone selfish who learns to care for others? A coward who discovers courage? Or maybe someone noble who's slowly broken down by the ugliness around them? Think about what the war will *do* to this person. That's your story arc. The war is the crucible—and your character is the metal being reshaped inside it.

Start by sketching out who your character is before the war touches them. What do they want? What do they fear? What defines their sense of self? Maybe they're a medic who believes in saving everyone. Maybe they're a soldier obsessed with glory. Maybe they're a pacifist who gets drafted. Maybe they're just a regular person trying to keep their family safe. You need to understand their foundation before you start breaking it. Knowing who they were gives weight to who they become. And it also makes the audience care. Nobody roots for a blank slate. They root for someone with flaws, strengths, beliefs, and vulnerabilities.

A powerful war drama protagonist doesn't need to be a traditional hero. In fact, the more human they are, the better. Give them contradictions. Let them make bad choices. Let them be scared, selfish, angry. But give them a sense of depth—something to hold onto. Maybe they're deeply loyal to a friend. Maybe they write poetry when no one's looking. Maybe they have a little superstition they cling to, like a lucky coin or a prayer they whisper under their breath. These small touches give your character texture, and they become even more powerful when the world around them starts to crumble.

Think about what your character wants at the beginning of the story. Not just in a general sense, but something specific. Maybe they want to return home. Maybe they want revenge. Maybe they want to protect someone. Maybe they want to prove they're brave. Then think about what the war will do to that want. Will it be fulfilled? Will it become irrelevant? Will it be replaced with something more important? A character who starts out wanting one thing and ends up needing something else—that's a story worth telling.

You also want to define your character's strengths. Not just in terms of skills, but in terms of emotional resilience. Are they calm under pressure? Are they good at inspiring others? Are they incredibly observant? These qualities will get tested. They'll be pushed to the limit. That's where the drama comes in. When you build a character who's good at something, you can then construct scenes that challenge or threaten that very strength. Maybe the calm leader finally cracks. Maybe the loyal friend is forced to betray someone. These reversals are what keep the story emotionally rich.

Don't forget their weaknesses. Every great character has at least one. Maybe they're impulsive. Maybe they're wracked with guilt. Maybe they freeze up in critical moments. Maybe they lie to protect themselves. These weaknesses should influence their decisions. They should cause real problems. The goal isn't to make your character perfect—it's to make them believable. In a war story, weakness is often what brings tension, and what sets up powerful turning points. When a flawed character is forced to face the thing they've been avoiding, you get unforgettable scenes.

The relationships your character has are just as important as their inner world. Who do they care about? Who do they owe something to? Who do they hate, and why? Maybe they have a brother in the same unit. Maybe they've made a promise to a dying friend. Maybe they're haunted by a commanding officer who doesn't care if they live or die. Relationships create stakes. When a character has something—or someone—to lose, their actions start to matter more. War is always personal. The big explosions are cool, but it's the look between two friends before one of them goes over the top that hits you in the heart.

ChatGPT is a great tool for character development at this stage. You can describe the basics of your character and ask the AI to help you build out their personality, history, and emotional journey. For example, you could say, "I'm writing a war drama about a young nurse in WWII who starts out naïve and hopeful—help me flesh out her personality and backstory," and see what it comes back with. You can ask for possible arcs, moral dilemmas, character flaws, even signature dialogue styles. Use the AI to help sharpen your ideas, not replace them.

Think about the moments that will define your character throughout the story. What are the turning points that change them forever? It could be a death, a betrayal, a rescue, a choice to abandon a mission to save a life. War provides constant opportunities for people to face the impossible. You want at least a few scenes that serve as emotional crossroads—moments where your character either becomes more of who they were, or starts to become someone entirely new. These are your emotional anchors. They show the audience who the character is, and who they're becoming.

And finally, think about how your story ends, and what your character's final moment says about them. Maybe they've survived, but they're broken. Maybe they've found peace, even in death. Maybe they've held onto hope, or maybe they've lost it entirely. That final image should feel like a reflection of everything they've been through. It's not just about whether they win or lose—it's about who they are in that last scene, and how different they are from the person we met in the beginning.

A powerful central character is the heart of any war drama. They don't have to be a soldier. They don't have to be brave. They just have to be human. They need to want something, struggle for it, and be changed by what they go through. When you get that right, everything else—plot, setting, theme—starts to come alive around them. So take your time with this character. Get to know them like they're real. Because once they're fully formed, they'll do something amazing—they'll take the lead, and the story will follow.

The Role of the Soldier in Your Story

If there's one figure most closely associated with war drama, it's the soldier. He or she is often the one on the front line, knee-deep in mud, hearing the snap of bullets and the thud of mortars, grappling with death in real time. But the role of the soldier in your story doesn't have to follow any expected pattern. A soldier can be the central protagonist, a background presence, a broken figure, a hero, a villain, or even a mirror to reflect the emotional state of the world you're building. What matters most is that the soldier in your war drama feels human, complex, and necessary to the emotional spine of the narrative.

There's a reason the soldier remains a timeless figure in storytelling—war strips people down. It brings out the best and the worst in them. And that intensity is where great drama lives. But not every soldier has to be Rambo or a wise-cracking veteran. The more specific and personal you make them, the more powerful your story becomes. Before you figure out what your soldier *does*, think about who they *are*. Where did they come from? Did they enlist or were they drafted? Are they fighting for a cause they believe in, or are they just trying to survive until it's over? Those small questions can lead to huge emotional payoffs.

In many stories, the soldier is the lens through which we experience the war. They might be confused, scared, uncertain—just like the reader or viewer. They're our entry point. They ask the same questions we do. Why is this happening? What's the point of it all? What am I supposed to do when the world's on fire? A soldier at the center of the story doesn't have to have the answers. In fact, the best ones usually don't. They just move forward, one painful decision at a time, and that quiet perseverance becomes the heartbeat of the entire story.

But you might not want the soldier to be the protagonist. And that's fine too. Soldiers in supporting roles can still be deeply important. Maybe your main character is a nurse, a journalist, or a civilian, and the soldier serves as a symbol of what's at stake. Maybe they represent the violence that's always just outside the door. Or maybe they're a source of strength, a protector, a threat, or even a love interest. The soldier's presence brings tension, and tension brings story. Even if they're not the lead, they can shift the emotional balance in every scene they appear in.

There's also the question of what kind of soldier you're writing. Are they trained and disciplined? Are they a raw recruit? Are they broken from what they've seen? Are they hardened and numb? Each version brings its own energy. A rookie is a great way to introduce the audience to the horrors of war—because they're learning and reacting as the audience does. A veteran gives you the chance to explore themes like desensitization, regret, or emotional detachment. A deserter adds a layer of conflict and danger. A soldier who can no longer follow orders opens up a moral minefield. Every variation gives you something to work with, something to challenge.

One of the best things you can do is give your soldier a contradiction. Maybe they're a tough-as-nails fighter who writes letters home in poetic verse. Maybe they're terrified in battle but incredibly brave when it comes to protecting others. Maybe they hate killing but are really good at it. These contradictions are what make characters feel real. They also give you room to explore deeper emotional moments when the story slows down. The quiet scenes are often just as powerful as the loud ones. A soldier cleaning their boots while humming an old song can say more than a hundred gunshots.

You should also think about what kind of unit or environment your soldier is in. Are they alone or part of a group? Are they leading others or following orders? Is their group tight-knit, or fractured and on the edge of collapse? The group dynamic around a soldier can be a huge source of conflict, loyalty, betrayal, humor, or tragedy. A soldier who loves his comrades but hates the war is already a deeply compelling character. A soldier who's trusted by some and doubted by others—now that's tension waiting to explode.

And then there's the mission. What is your soldier trying to achieve? Are they on patrol? Escorting civilians? Trying to find a way home? Sent on a doomed mission that nobody believes in? The mission defines the shape of your plot, but it also reveals character. How they handle setbacks, danger, or loss shows the reader who they really are. A soldier under fire is one thing—but a soldier making impossible choices under fire, that's where your story gets its teeth.

Using ChatGPT, you can generate soldiers with full backstories and emotional profiles. You can prompt it with something like, "Create a soldier character who is conflicted about the war but deeply loyal to his platoon," and then keep refining until you've got someone who feels real. You can ask for key moments in their life, potential emotional arcs, or even sample dialogue. Don't just settle for stock characters. Dig deep until you find someone who surprises you.

Another angle to consider is what happens to your soldier *after* the war—or during the quiet moments in between the battles. Do they carry guilt? Do they lose their sense of identity? Are they searching for redemption or peace? These questions help extend your story beyond just the action. They give your war drama emotional gravity. Because at the end of the day, a good war story isn't about how many battles someone survives—it's about what those battles do to their soul.

The soldier in your story should never be a cardboard cut-out. Make them bleed. Make them laugh. Make them regret. Let them want things they can't have, remember people they've lost, and fear things they won't admit. Let them be brave and broken in the same breath. Because that's what war does to people—it complicates them, tests them, and, if they're lucky, transforms them.

Whether your soldier is front and center or on the edges of the frame, make sure they matter. Make sure their story feels real, even if everything around them is fiction. Because when the bullets stop flying and the credits roll or the final page turns, what people remember won't be the explosions. They'll remember the person who walked through them—and what it cost to keep walking.

Writing From the Civilian Perspective

When people think about war dramas, their minds often go straight to the battlefield—soldiers charging, bullets flying, bombs dropping. But some of the most powerful and emotionally resonant war stories don't come from the trenches at all. They come from kitchens, bomb shelters, refugee camps, empty streets, and crowded trains. They come from the voices of civilians—ordinary people caught in the crossfire of something they didn't start, can't control, and may never understand. Writing from the civilian perspective opens up a different dimension of the war drama, one that's quieter but just as harrowing, and sometimes even more heartbreaking.

The civilian perspective is the story of survival without weapons. It's about endurance without power. It's about navigating a world where danger is everywhere, but the means to fight back are few. When you write a civilian character into your war drama, you're giving the audience a window into the emotional cost of war—the trauma that lingers long after the battles are over. Civilians represent the collateral damage, the ones who suffer in silence, who bury their loved ones and rebuild their homes while the rest of the world moves on.

This perspective works beautifully for character-driven storytelling. Civilians don't usually have a military mission or objective to follow, so their stories are guided by emotion, relationship, and daily survival. That gives you the freedom to focus on more intimate moments—grief, resilience, kindness, fear, small victories. A grandmother hiding a neighbor from the occupying force. A child trying to make sense of why their world is crumbling. A shopkeeper who becomes a resistance leader after losing everything. These are the kinds of characters that stick with people, not because they were the strongest or the smartest, but because they were real.

Writing from this angle also gives you access to a broader range of characters. You can write about mothers and fathers, lovers and friends, old people and children, people from every background, class, and ideology. You're not limited to the standard military roles. You get to show how war affects families, communities, schools, and entire cities. You get to show how people try to hold on to a sense of normalcy in the middle of chaos—cooking meals, telling stories, falling in love, hiding in basements. These moments might be small, but they can carry an enormous emotional punch.

And let's not forget tension. Civilians in wartime are often at the mercy of larger, unseen forces. That creates incredible suspense. They might be hiding someone. They might be trying to escape. They might be suspected of something they didn't do. They might be living under constant threat, walking a tightrope of pretending to comply while secretly resisting. Every conversation can be dangerous. Every knock on the door can change everything. That kind of tension doesn't require a single gunshot—it's baked into the setting.

The civilian story is also perfect for exploring themes like displacement, memory, trauma, identity, resistance, and forgiveness. These stories can be slow burns, focusing on how war changes people over time, how communities fracture or come together, how individuals discover reserves of strength they never knew they had. These themes are universal. Not everyone has served in a war, but almost everyone can relate to the fear of losing a loved one, the helplessness of watching things fall apart, the need to protect something precious.

You can also use the civilian perspective to give your war drama moral depth. Civilians don't always understand the big picture of the war. They see the impact but not the strategy. That allows you to show how messy and confusing war really is. You can challenge the idea of heroes and villains. You can show soldiers through the eyes of those who fear them—or those who admire them. You can explore what it means to survive when others fight in your name. That moral ambiguity is powerful, and it makes for complex, unforgettable characters.

This perspective also allows for stories that cross paths with the war rather than being immersed in it from beginning to end. Maybe your story takes place before the bombs fall, and the tension is in not knowing when life will change. Maybe it takes place after the war ends, in the ruins and silence, where the real work of healing begins. Civilians live the entire arc of a war—the buildup, the explosion, the aftermath. You can set your story at any point in that arc and still find rich emotional territory to explore.

Use ChatGPT to help develop civilian characters who feel real. Ask for ideas about people living in occupied cities, or families torn apart by forced relocation, or children dealing with the psychological aftermath of bombings. You can create profiles, generate backstories, or ask for examples of daily life under specific historical conditions. The AI can even help you brainstorm the little details—what kind of food they eat, how they travel, what they hear on the radio, what rumours spread through the streets.

One of the most effective techniques when writing from a civilian perspective is to show the contrast between the normal and the horrific. A woman hanging laundry while distant shelling echoes in the background. A child playing in the rubble of what used to be a home. A teacher trying to keep a classroom together while the war closes in. These juxtapositions create powerful emotional moments, showing how war creeps into every corner of life. It's not always about direct violence. Sometimes the tragedy is in the way life continues even when everything is falling apart.

If you're writing a war story and you feel like you've seen the soldier's journey a hundred times, the civilian perspective might be the shift that unlocks something new. It gives you a chance to write about fear and bravery in quieter, subtler ways. It lets you show the cost of war from the ground up. It centers your story on the human experience rather than the strategic one.

In the end, writing from the civilian perspective is about honoring the millions of lives that are reshaped, scarred, or lost in wars they didn't choose. It's about looking beyond the battlefield and asking what it means to survive, to adapt, to love, and to keep going in a world that no longer makes sense. Whether you're writing a novel, a screenplay, or a short story, this perspective can make your war drama more layered, more nuanced, and more deeply felt. Because sometimes, the most powerful stories aren't about those who fight—but about those who endure.

War through the Eyes of the Enemy

One of the boldest and most powerful decisions you can make when writing a war drama is to tell the story through the eyes of the enemy. It's uncomfortable. It's challenging. And that's exactly why it can be so compelling. In most war stories, the enemy is a shadow—an unseen threat, a faceless figure, a target. But war isn't made of shadows. It's made of people. And writing from the perspective of the other side, whoever they are, forces your audience to face the truth that the enemy has a name, a family, fears, regrets, and sometimes the same goals as your heroes.

This doesn't mean turning a blind eye to atrocities or rewriting history to suit a new narrative. It means digging into the complexity of human beings caught in war, regardless of which side they're on. When you show war through the eyes of the enemy, you're not condoning their side—you're humanizing the war. And that humanization creates an emotional tension that makes your story more real, more nuanced, and more unforgettable.

Start by asking yourself who the enemy is in your story. Maybe it's a soldier from the other side, a general leading the opposition, a young conscript who never wanted to fight. Maybe it's someone in a government office pushing buttons from afar. Or maybe it's someone who doesn't even see themselves as the enemy at all—they believe they're the hero. That belief, that disconnect between perception and reality, is rich soil for drama. A character who thinks they're saving their people while destroying others can be incredibly compelling—and incredibly tragic.

Perspective is everything. Let's say your story is about the Allied forces storming a beach. You could write it from the perspective of a German soldier stationed in a bunker, terrified, conflicted, just trying to survive. Maybe he believes he's protecting his homeland. Maybe he's starting to realize the lies he was told. Maybe he has a brother fighting on the Eastern Front and he's just trying to live long enough to see him again. Suddenly, the entire scene shifts. It's no longer just about good guys and bad guys—it's about two terrified men, caught in a machine that doesn't care about either of them.

This kind of storytelling demands empathy—not sympathy, not agreement, but the willingness to understand. You don't need to justify the enemy's actions. But you do need to explore *why* they act the way they do. What were they taught? What pressures are they under? What are they afraid of losing? Once you start answering those questions, your character starts to breathe. And the war begins to feel bigger, sadder, and more human.

The enemy perspective is especially useful when you want to explore themes like propaganda, brainwashing, nationalism, guilt, or redemption. You can show how ideology infects people over time, how fear shapes behavior, how good people can end up on the wrong side of history. These are tough, emotionally complex ideas—but they're also where the most meaningful stories live.

One of the great advantages of writing war through the eyes of the enemy is the opportunity for reversal. Maybe your enemy character begins loyal and confident in their cause, only to watch it unravel. Maybe they meet someone from the other side who changes their mind. Maybe they commit a terrible act and spend the rest of the story trying to atone. Or maybe they never change at all, and that in itself becomes the tragedy. When your audience is waiting for redemption and doesn't get it, that absence can hit just as hard as any emotional payoff.

There's also the shock factor. When you take your audience inside the life of someone they're trained to dislike, you force them to confront their own assumptions. You ask them to feel compassion where they didn't expect to. And when done right, that emotional discomfort turns into insight. It breaks down the idea that war is clean and simple. It tears away the illusion that heroism is only found on one side of the line.

ChatGPT can help you craft these characters carefully. You can start with a prompt like, "Create a morally conflicted enemy soldier who begins to question their role in the war," and see what kinds of details emerge. You can explore cultural background, personal motivations, family life, religion, education—anything that adds complexity. Use the AI to generate possible emotional arcs, key turning points, or ethical dilemmas that would make your enemy character feel real.

When writing from this perspective, be mindful of the historical and emotional weight your story carries. If you're writing about a real conflict, especially one involving war crimes or genocide, it's essential to approach the material with respect and responsibility. You're not excusing anything. You're opening a door to emotional complexity. And that means doing your research, understanding the context, and making sure your character's inner world reflects the tension and turmoil of someone living on the wrong side of history.

There's also room to explore imagined conflicts through this lens. In a fictional war or alternate history, you can build an enemy culture from the ground up and then drop your character into it. Maybe they grew up in a militarized society. Maybe their family was destroyed by the war. Maybe they've been taught that the other side is evil since they were born. You can use this to explore broader ideas—about fear, control, identity, or the thin line between loyalty and indoctrination. In fiction, the enemy perspective becomes a mirror held up to our own world, asking hard questions in ways that don't feel preachy.

You don't have to tell your whole story through this point of view, either. Sometimes the most powerful effect comes from slipping into the enemy's head for a chapter or a scene. Giving them a moment of vulnerability. Letting the audience feel what they feel. That shift can be jarring—and deeply moving. Even if your main protagonist is fighting against them, seeing the enemy as more than a monster deepens the emotional resonance of every encounter.

At its heart, writing from the enemy's perspective is about storytelling with courage. It means refusing to flatten your characters into good guys and bad guys. It means understanding that in war, everyone loses something. Everyone bleeds. And sometimes, the only difference between the hero and the enemy is the uniform they were handed.

So ask yourself—what happens if we look through the other side's eyes? What do we learn? What do we feel? What truths do we uncover? Because once you give the enemy a voice, you're not just writing a war drama. You're writing a human story—one with the power to challenge, change, and endure.

Creating the Ensemble Cast

War drama thrives on more than just one central character. While a single protagonist can guide the emotional core of your story, the world of war is too vast, too chaotic, and too emotionally charged to be fully understood through one set of eyes. That's where the ensemble cast comes in. A well-crafted ensemble not only gives your story depth and variety—it creates contrast, conflict, and connection. It builds a world where multiple voices clash, harmonize, and evolve. In a war drama, the ensemble is the chorus of humanity. And it's your job to make each voice matter.

Creating an ensemble doesn't mean simply throwing in a bunch of characters and hoping they stick. Each one should serve a purpose. Each one should reflect a different aspect of the war. Some might echo your protagonist's beliefs. Others might challenge them. Some will survive. Some won't. The magic of the ensemble is that it allows the audience to see how different kinds of people experience the same event. A young recruit, an old veteran, a reluctant fighter, an adrenaline junkie, a medic with a pacifist heart, a cynic who jokes to survive, a leader on the verge of collapse—these kinds of characters create a tapestry of perspectives that bring the war to life.

When building your ensemble, start with your protagonist. Who are they? What's their emotional arc? Now build out from there. Create characters who will help shape that journey. Maybe someone who mentors them. Maybe someone who antagonizes them. Maybe someone who mirrors them, showing what they could become or what they used to be. These relationships form the emotional architecture of your story. The war might be the plot, but the people are the glue.

Each character should have their own small arc. It doesn't have to be big or dramatic. Sometimes it's a quiet change—a belief lost, a friendship formed, a truth uncovered. Other times, it's a full transformation. The cocky soldier learns humility. The fearful one finds courage. The jaded one rediscovers their humanity. These arcs don't just serve the individual characters—they enrich your main narrative by creating emotional rhythm. Moments of tension, humor, sadness, and hope rise and fall through the ensemble.

Personality contrast is key. Don't create five characters who all talk the same, think the same, and act the same. Think about personality archetypes, and then push them into unique territory. If you've got a stoic, maybe pair them with someone who can't stop talking. If you've got a by-the-book soldier, introduce someone who bends every rule. These contrasts naturally generate tension and spark dynamic scenes. And in war, where life and death often depend on collaboration, these differences become battlegrounds of their own.

Think about cultural, social, and regional diversity. War is a great equalizer, but people don't enter it from the same starting point. A street-smart kid from the Bronx and a farm boy from Iowa are going to see the battlefield in completely different ways. A French partisan, a Soviet tank driver, and a German defecting from his post—each brings a unique lens to the experience of war. Diversity of background deepens your story and makes your world feel authentic. It also invites readers to connect with the story through multiple emotional entry points.

The ensemble cast is also an incredible tool for pacing. When your story slows down, shift perspective. When your protagonist is emotionally stuck, let another character's arc move the story forward. When the tension in one plotline needs a break, cut to a different emotional beat. A well-balanced ensemble gives you flexibility without losing focus. Each subplot becomes a tributary feeding into the river of your main story.

Use ChatGPT to help brainstorm your ensemble. You can give it your story's main concept and ask, "What kinds of characters would naturally form around this protagonist in a WWII bomber squad?" or "Give me character ideas for a group of resistance fighters in occupied France." Then take those ideas and twist them. Add contradictions. If you've got a character who's a priest, make him a priest who secretly sabotages trains. If you've got a mechanic, give her a background in philosophy. You want people who surprise the reader—not because they're unrealistic, but because they feel like actual humans with layers.

Dialogue is where the ensemble really comes to life. When each character has a clear voice—tone, rhythm, vocabulary—you don't even need to tag who's speaking. You just know. That kind of character clarity takes time, but it's worth it. Dialogue in war dramas is often where the emotional truth breaks through. The joking around the fire. The whispered confessions in the dark. The shouted arguments when tension snaps. These moments stick because they remind us that, underneath the uniform, everyone's just trying to make sense of the madness.

And don't be afraid to let your ensemble suffer. Loss, betrayal, injury, disappearance—all of it. War is cruel, and your audience knows not everyone will make it. But when you've built strong characters who matter to the reader, those moments of loss hit like a gut punch. They raise the stakes. They create silence where there used to be laughter. And they remind your protagonist—and the reader—that nothing in war is guaranteed.

Your ensemble also gives you a way to explore themes from multiple angles. One character might represent hope, another futility. One might believe in the cause, another might see the war as pointless. Through them, you don't have to preach or explain your themes. You show them. You let the reader feel the moral ambiguity, the emotional highs and lows, and the personal contradictions that war brings out in people.

By the time you reach the final scenes, your ensemble should feel like a memory—real, flawed, unforgettable people who walked through hell together. Maybe only a few remain. Maybe none do. But their voices echo in the protagonist's decisions, in the emotional texture of the final image, in the reader's heart. They gave the war a face. They gave it soul. And that's what great ensemble casts do.

So when you're building your war drama, don't just fill the background with bodies. Fill it with people. Let them live, argue, laugh, break, dream, and fight. Let them matter to each other—and to your audience. Because when the last bullet has been fired and the final scene fades to black, it's the ensemble we remember. Not the war itself, but the people who lived through it. Or didn't.

Understanding Military Ranks and Roles

If you're writing a war drama and you want your world to feel authentic, one of the things you need to get a handle on early is military ranks and roles. You don't need to become a military historian or memorize every insignia from every army that ever existed—but you do need to know how the chain of command works and how different soldiers function within it. The military is a rigid, structured world, and if you're not careful, it's easy to write characters who are in the wrong place, giving the wrong orders, or performing jobs that don't match their rank. When the structure makes sense, your war story becomes more immersive. When it doesn't, it breaks the illusion fast.

Military ranks exist for a reason. In war, chaos is everywhere—bullets are flying, people are dying, plans are changing by the minute. Without a clear hierarchy, everything would fall apart. That hierarchy determines who gives orders, who takes them, and who's responsible when things go wrong. So if your story involves soldiers, you need to understand where each one stands on that ladder. Who leads the squad? Who runs the platoon? Who's in command at the battalion level? If you get that right, everything else—dialogue, decisions, tension—starts to feel grounded in reality.

Let's break it down simply. Most militaries are divided into enlisted personnel and officers. Enlisted personnel are the backbone—the soldiers, medics, mechanics, gunners, and everyone else doing the on-the-ground work. Officers are the leaders, planners, and decision-makers. Within these categories, there's a clear hierarchy. In the U.S. Army, for example, a Private is the lowest enlisted rank, and a General is the highest officer rank. In between, you've got ranks like Corporal, Sergeant, Lieutenant, Captain, Major, Colonel, and so on. Each one comes with different responsibilities and authority levels.

So let's say you're writing about a small squad of soldiers in WWII. The squad is probably led by a Sergeant or Staff Sergeant. This character gives orders in the field, makes tactical decisions, and keeps the group together. Above the squad level, a Lieutenant or Captain might be in charge of a platoon made up of several squads. A Major or Colonel might command a company or battalion. If your story is focused on small-unit dynamics—tight-knit groups under fire—then knowing this hierarchy helps you understand who's in charge and who's vulnerable. It also gives your characters real stakes when orders are followed, challenged, or ignored.

Rank also influences how characters talk to each other. A Private isn't going to casually backtalk a Lieutenant in the middle of a mission—unless they're at a breaking point, and that creates drama. A Sergeant might argue with a Captain behind closed doors but would show respect in front of the troops. Military culture is full of unspoken rules, customs, and expectations around authority, obedience, and respect. When you understand those dynamics, you can use them to build tension. A character stepping out of line might be punished, demoted, or even court-martialled. Or they might be secretly admired for their defiance, depending on the situation. The role someone plays is just as important as their rank. Every soldier isn't a rifleman. Some are medics. Some are engineers. Some are snipers, radio operators, tank drivers, intelligence officers, mechanics, supply clerks. A high-ranking officer might never see combat but plays a crucial role in strategy or logistics. A low-ranking soldier might be carrying out missions that have massive consequences. When assigning roles to your characters, think about how those jobs affect their worldview. A medic sees the wounded and dying up close. A supply officer worries about food and ammunition. A sniper is often alone, isolated, calculating. A radio operator has to stay calm under pressure and keep communication flowing. These roles aren't just technical—they're emotional landscapes.

You can use ChatGPT to help sort through the possibilities. If your story is set in a specific time and place, like the Korean War or a future space conflict, ask for a breakdown of typical military units, command structure, and roles. You can generate realistic combinations, like a Sergeant leading a reconnaissance unit or a Corporal in charge of demolition. You can ask what kind of training they'd have, what equipment they'd use, and what kind of orders they'd be expected to carry out. This kind of research gives your story credibility—and helps you avoid writing something that takes the audience out of the world you're building.

The chain of command can also create natural story tension. Orders come down from the top—but what happens when those orders don't make sense on the ground? Maybe a General sitting in a bunker is ordering an advance that the Lieutenant on the field knows will be a slaughter. Now you've got conflict. Does the officer disobey and save lives? Or follow orders and risk everything? These moments of hierarchy vs. morality are perfect for character development. You're not just showing a rank structure—you're testing it.

Rank can also be symbolic. A soldier who refuses a promotion might be avoiding responsibility or haunted by survivor's guilt. A young officer given command might struggle with insecurity or impostor syndrome. A grizzled veteran who never moved up might have chosen to stay close to the action—or been kept down for political reasons. Use rank to reveal personality, history, and inner conflict. A title is more than a job. It's a weight your character carries, whether they earned it, inherited it, or resent it.

Think about how your characters interact based on their place in the structure. Who has the power to give orders? Who carries the consequences? Who has authority but doubts themselves? Who has no authority but commands respect anyway? These questions shape how your characters behave under stress—and war is nothing but stress. When a Private saves a Sergeant's life, how does that shift the dynamic? When a Lieutenant leads men into a trap, how does that affect morale? When a General's decision kills civilians, who speaks up?

Military ranks and roles don't have to dominate your story, but they need to support it. They're part of the scaffolding that holds up the drama. If your readers or viewers feel like the world follows rules, they'll be more willing to believe in the emotions, relationships, and consequences you're showing them. If the world feels sloppy or inconsistent, everything else gets shaky too. So take the time to understand how military structure works. Use it to inform your character relationships, your scenes of conflict, your moments of tension. Use it to heighten stakes, create reversals, and explore loyalty and disobedience. Because when war breaks out in your story, and people start making impossible decisions, the ranks on their shoulders and the roles they've been given will shape every moment of what happens next.

Building Character Backstories in Times of War

In any story, a well-built character backstory adds emotional weight to every scene. But in a war drama, that backstory does something more—it becomes the quiet battlefield your character carries within. Before the first bullet is fired or the first siren screams, your characters had lives. They had families, dreams, wounds, and regrets. War doesn't erase that history—it exposes it. It forces it to the surface and asks, "Who are you, really, when everything is falling apart?" When you build character backstories in times of war, you're not just creating context—you're loading the emotional gun.

Backstory is more than a list of facts. It's about who your characters were before the war found them. Maybe your protagonist was a schoolteacher. A farmer. A thief. A poet. Maybe they never held a weapon before the war. Maybe they've never known a world without it. Their past shapes their reactions. A character who grew up in a peaceful home might freeze the first time they hear gunfire. Someone raised in hardship might adapt faster, but carry their trauma more quietly. Every decision your character makes during the war is filtered through who they were before it.

Start with the basics—where did your character come from? Not just the town or country, but the emotional geography. What kind of environment shaped them? Were they raised in wealth or poverty? Were they loved or neglected? Were they told who to be, or did they have to figure it out alone? These elements matter because war will strip them back to their core. A character with something to lose behaves differently from one who never had anything in the first place. A character who believed in fairness might fall apart when war exposes the world's cruelty.

Family is a great place to mine for emotional complexity. Are they trying to get back to someone? Are they haunted by someone they lost? Do they carry guilt for something they said—or didn't say—before the war began? Maybe they're fighting for a sibling who was taken. Maybe they don't know what happened to their child. Maybe they were disowned for enlisting or despised for refusing to. These are the things that follow them through the story, whispered in their thoughts even as bombs explode around them. Use family as a tether to the past. It keeps your characters grounded even as the world spins out of control.

Also think about beliefs. Before the war, what did they believe about right and wrong? About their country, their enemies, their place in the world? What did they trust in? Religion, politics, people, fate? These beliefs don't have to be static. In fact, one of the most powerful arcs in war drama is watching a belief system slowly crack, bend, or break under pressure. A soldier who starts the war convinced of their side's righteousness might begin to see the rot beneath the surface. A pacifist forced to kill might never look in the mirror the same way again. When beliefs clash with necessity, the emotional sparks fly.

Don't overlook the small things. Backstory isn't just about trauma and ideology. It's about detail. What was their favorite song? Their favorite meal? What did they want to be before the war? Did they have a crush on someone? A hobby they were great at? A pet they left behind? These seemingly minor details become emotional anchors later. They come up in quiet moments—in a joke told around the fire, a memory shared while hiding in a trench, a name muttered in sleep. These small things give your character dimension. They make the reader care.

And then there's the secret. Almost every powerful war drama character carries one. Something they did. Something they didn't do. Something they're ashamed of or trying to forget. Secrets are dynamite for character tension. Maybe they forged papers. Maybe they betrayed someone. Maybe they didn't save a friend. Maybe they're not who they say they are. Secrets fuel conflict within the group, drive inner turmoil, and can explode at the worst possible time. They make your character unpredictable. And that makes them unforgettable.

You can use ChatGPT to generate detailed backstories quickly. Just feed in the basic idea of your character and ask the AI to expand. Try, "Give me a backstory for a soldier in the Korean War who used to be a jazz musician," or "Create a past for a WWII nurse who lost her fiancé in the Blitz." You can then refine that with emotional arcs, specific memories, and personality traits shaped by the pre-war life. Let the AI help you fill in those layers—but don't stop at surface-level facts. Keep digging until something makes your character feel real to you.

One technique that helps is writing a flashback scene before you begin your main story. Place your character at home, at work, at school—anywhere pre-war. Let them interact with the world when it's still normal. This doesn't have to appear in the final script or manuscript, but it gives you a strong emotional foundation. Now, when you drop that same character into a battlefield or a ruined city, you—and your audience—feel the weight of what they've lost.

Backstory also helps you manage the emotional pacing of your story. When the plot is moving fast—explosions, escapes, gunfights—it's easy to forget that the characters need space to breathe. That's where backstory comes in. A quiet scene, a memory shared, a photo pulled from a helmet—these are the moments where the heart of your story beats. They let the reader exhale. They remind everyone that these aren't just soldiers or survivors—they're people with stories behind their eyes.

And backstory doesn't have to come all at once. In fact, it's better if it doesn't. Let it drip out. A line here. A detail there. Let the past emerge when the present calls for it. When a character sees a dog and remembers the one they left behind. When they hear a song and think of the girl they danced with before deployment. These quiet echoes make your war story feel alive with memory—and that's where the emotional depth comes from.

War doesn't create people. It reveals them. And the person being revealed in your story needs to have a history, even if most of it stays in the background. Build that history with care. Let it inform your dialogue, your decisions, your emotional arcs. Because when the bullets start flying and the world turns upside down, it's the past your character clings to, runs from, or desperately tries to remember. And that past is what makes them real—not just to you, but to every reader or viewer who follows them into the heart of war.

Creating Authentic Dialogue under Fire

Writing dialogue during battle scenes is one of the most delicate balancing acts in a war drama. Get it right, and your characters feel alive, their relationships shine through the chaos, and the emotion of the moment hits with brutal impact. Get it wrong, and everything starts to feel forced, overly dramatic, or worse—inauthentic. Creating believable, impactful dialogue under fire is about more than just what characters say. It's about how they speak when everything is on the line, when fear, adrenaline, and confusion all come crashing in at once.

The first thing to remember is that in the middle of combat, nobody's delivering monologues. This is not the time for poetic speeches or long-winded backstories. When bullets are flying and lives are in danger, people speak in short bursts, clipped sentences, even single words. Dialogue becomes functional—shouted warnings, urgent commands, guttural reactions. The pressure of the moment strips language down to its barest form. "Incoming!" "Left side!" "Move!" These words aren't just about clarity—they're about survival.

But even within that stripped-down language, emotion still seeps through. A barked command can be laced with desperation. A sarcastic one-liner can be a defense mechanism against fear. The way a character says something is just as important as the words they use. One soldier might scream orders with panic in their voice, while another speaks with eerie calm, revealing how they cope under pressure. Use tone to add emotional depth, even in the most frantic scenes.

Then there's the dynamic between characters. Even in chaos, relationships don't disappear. A friend calling out for a wounded comrade, a leader trying to calm their squad, a soldier cracking a joke to break the tension—these interactions show who these people are beneath the armor. These moments can be quick, but they're powerful. A shared look, a name screamed across a battlefield, a whispered "Stay with me" as someone bleeds—these are the emotional punches that stay with your audience long after the dust settles.

One of the most effective tools you can use is contrast. Not all dialogue during a firefight needs to be about the fight itself. Sometimes the most human thing your characters can do is talk about something totally unrelated. A soldier talking about the meal they're going to eat if they survive. Someone arguing about baseball scores while ducking gunfire. These moments of normalcy in the middle of madness create tension and show how people use conversation to hold onto their sanity. They also reveal character in unexpected ways.

Authentic dialogue also reflects the natural rhythm of military communication. Depending on the branch, the unit, and the era, language will sound different. WWII soldiers spoke differently than modern-day Marines. British troops don't use the same slang as American ones. A special forces team communicates differently than a platoon of conscripts. Do a bit of research into the slang, shorthand, and tone of speech used by real soldiers in your setting. ChatGPT can help here—ask for typical military slang from a specific war or unit, and see how the language can add texture to your scenes.

Be careful not to overuse profanity or military jargon just to sound "authentic." Yes, real soldiers swear. A lot. And yes, they use abbreviations and lingo. But if every sentence is packed with obscure terms or relentless cursing, the emotional clarity of the scene can get lost. Choose your moments. A well-placed curse can be powerful. Too many, and it starts to sound like you're trying too hard. Let the characters speak the way real people speak under stress—fast, sharp, imperfect, but full of feeling.

One challenge many writers face is balancing chaos and clarity. During intense action, you want the reader or viewer to feel disoriented—but not confused. Dialogue can help orient the audience. A shouted command lets us know which way the threat is coming from. A scream of pain signals who's been hit. A soldier calling for backup reminds us that things are going badly. Use dialogue to plant narrative markers in the chaos—guide the reader without slowing down the pace.

Silence is also a kind of dialogue. Don't feel the need to fill every moment with chatter. Sometimes a glance, a clenched jaw, or the sound of breathing says more than any line of dialogue ever could. A character who says nothing in a firefight might be in shock, might be repressing panic, or might be laser-focused on staying alive. That silence can be louder than words. Use it strategically.

If you want to practice, try writing the same battle scene three different ways: one with functional military dialogue only, one with emotional reactions only, and one that blends both. Then compare the versions. Which one feels the most real? Which one gives you chills? Which one sounds like the people you're trying to portray? You can also use ChatGPT to simulate scenes with different dialogue tones—ask for "a battle scene with tense, clipped dialogue" or "a firefight where two characters argue while under fire." Use those results as a base, then add your personal touch.

Remember that dialogue under fire is where humanity and horror meet. It's where fear and love, duty and desperation, all come to the surface in fractured, shouted, half-breathed lines. It's not about cleverness. It's about emotional truth. If a soldier has one last thing to say before the lights go out, what would it be? If someone sees their best friend hit, what instinctive words come out of their mouth? If a leader knows the mission's gone wrong but has to keep the team moving, how do they do it with nothing but their voice?

In the end, creating authentic dialogue under fire is about capturing the heartbeat of survival. It's about showing how people hold on to each other, to life, to hope, with words that sometimes fail and sometimes save. And when it's done right, it doesn't just make the scene feel real—it makes the war feel personal. It makes your story unforgettable.

Setting the Emotional Tone of Your War Drama

The emotional tone of your war drama is like the blood in its veins—it flows through every moment, every scene, every line of dialogue. It's the feeling your audience carries from start to finish, whether it's dread, sorrow, rage, hope, or some haunting blend of them all. Tone isn't just about style or mood. It's about emotional honesty. When you set the right tone, everything else—the plot, the characters, the pacing—falls into place. Your story begins to breathe on its own. And when that happens, your war drama doesn't just inform or entertain. It leaves a mark.

Before you dive into writing scenes or planning battles, ask yourself: *What do I want the audience to feel from beginning to end?* That might sound simple, but it's one of the most important creative decisions you'll make. Are you telling a bleak, harrowing story about the futility of war? Are you writing a redemptive arc about healing and forgiveness? Is your story meant to feel raw and claustrophobic, or wide and epic? Is it fast and adrenaline-fueled or slow and meditative? The emotional tone you choose will shape every creative choice that follows.

Start by thinking about your core theme. If your war drama is about loss, the tone might be quiet, mournful, even poetic. If it's about survival, the tone might be urgent and tense, punctuated by moments of release. If it's about brotherhood, you might weave warmth and camaraderie through the cold violence of war. If your story is about disillusionment, the tone might start out bright and hopeful and slowly decay into something darker and more bitter. Emotional tone is fluid, but the emotional spine of your story should stay consistent—even as your characters evolve.

The setting contributes a lot to the emotional tone. A war fought in freezing mountains will feel very different from one fought in jungle heat or city ruins. Harsh weather, darkness, sound, and isolation—all of these environmental details carry emotional weight. You're not just describing scenery. You're creating a mood. Imagine the opening shot: fog rolls over a shattered forest. Crows pick at bodies in the snow. Or maybe it's a crowded train station, loud with shouting, children crying, soldiers kissing loved ones goodbye. That opening image sets the tone—and once you establish it, everything else builds from there.

Characters play a huge role in maintaining your tone. How they talk, react, and carry themselves in the face of violence or loss reflects the emotional world you're trying to create. A character who jokes constantly under fire gives your story a different rhythm than one who stays quiet and grim. A protagonist who's emotionally numb adds a cold, detached quality. A character who clings to faith or family adds hope to even the darkest moment. Use your ensemble to layer tone. Each voice in the group adds a different note—humor, heartbreak, fear, rage, resilience—and when balanced right, they create an emotional harmony.

Music and sound also play into tone, especially if you're writing for screen. Think about how scenes would *feel* with music layered underneath. A slow piano in a war-torn church. A single violin over a funeral. Or silence—sometimes the most powerful sound of all. Even if you're writing a novel, imagine the soundtrack. It can help you feel your way into the right rhythm for your story. The same battle scene can feel heroic, tragic, or terrifying depending on the emotional framing.

Tone also lives in pacing. A fast-paced story filled with constant conflict might feel chaotic, even breathless. That can be effective if your theme is about panic or survival. But if you want to explore trauma, regret, or healing, you'll need to slow down. Give your characters room to reflect. Let scenes linger. Show what happens in the pauses between battles—the quiet nights, the waiting, the drinking, the breakdowns. Those spaces are where the emotional weight sinks in. Don't rush through them. Let the tone stretch out and soak into the reader.

One way to keep your tone consistent is to choose a point-of-view character whose emotional state mirrors the world you're creating. If your protagonist is lost, scared, and unsure, and your story is told through their eyes, the tone will naturally reflect that confusion and fear. If they're angry and determined, the story will carry that fire. You don't have to constantly *describe* how the character feels—just let the tone of their thoughts, reactions, and decisions guide the reader's emotional response.

Use ChatGPT to test tonal variations. You can give it a scene prompt like "a soldier saying goodbye to his family before deployment" and ask it to write it in three tones—hopeful, tragic, and tense. You'll see how tone shifts word choice, rhythm, imagery, and emotional intensity. You can then apply that knowledge to your own writing, shaping each scene to align with your overall emotional vision.

Don't be afraid to contrast tones within a story, as long as the shifts serve a purpose. Moments of dark humor in a grim story can actually make the bleakness hit harder. A sudden quiet moment in an action-heavy sequence can magnify its emotional impact. A tender flashback before a character dies gives their loss more weight. Just make sure the shifts feel intentional and emotionally grounded. If the tone veers too wildly without reason, the audience might feel disoriented or disconnected.

The emotional tone you set will also determine the final note your story hits. That last scene, that final image, that closing line—it needs to feel like the natural conclusion to the tone you've been building. If your story has been brutal and uncompromising, a too-hopeful ending might ring false. If your story has held onto a thread of light through the darkness, a moment of peace or reunion might feel earned. The end should feel inevitable, not because the plot demands it, but because the emotional tone has led us there all along.

Ultimately, the emotional tone of your war drama is your contract with the audience. You're telling them, from page one or frame one, how to feel. You're inviting them into a world of pain, courage, chaos, or grace—and you're promising to guide them through it. Whether they emerge devastated, uplifted, haunted, or hopeful depends on how well you've shaped that emotional journey. So trust your instincts. Write from a place of emotional truth. And let your tone carry the weight of everything your characters can't always say out loud. That's how a war drama doesn't just tell a story—it makes people feel it in their bones.

The War Setting as a Character

In a war drama, the setting isn't just where things happen—it *is* something that happens. The war itself becomes a presence, an antagonist, a silent force shaping every decision, every emotion, every relationship. If you treat your setting like a character, it gains emotional weight. It interacts with your characters. It changes them. It watches, punishes, and sometimes offers moments of unexpected grace. The setting in a war drama is not passive. It's alive. And when you write it that way, your story becomes immersive in a way that facts and figures alone never could.

Think of the war setting not as a backdrop, but as a breathing, evolving entity. It has moods. It changes over time. It presses down on your characters like gravity. Whether your story unfolds in the scorched ruins of a city, a jungle so thick it swallows sound, a frozen battlefield where frostbite is as deadly as bullets, or a village caught between two advancing armies, your setting should feel like it has intention. Like it knows something your characters don't. Like it's always watching.

Let's say your story takes place in a bombed-out town. That place isn't just rubble. It's memory. Every collapsed building was once a home. Every empty window is a pair of eyes. Every street, once full of life, is now haunted. That emotional residue is part of your story. You can show it through the way your characters move, the things they notice, the places they avoid. Maybe they pause before stepping over a doll in the dirt. Maybe they recognize a smell that brings back a life they lost. When you embed emotional echoes into the environment, your setting becomes a character with a backstory—and that deepens the audience's connection.

Or maybe your war drama takes place on the front lines, where the setting shifts day by day. Trenches flood. Trees are splintered by artillery. Smoke turns the sun orange. The geography itself starts to reflect the psychological state of the characters. A hill becomes cursed because too many friends died trying to take it. A river means danger because it's where the enemy crossed last time. Places gain meaning as the war unfolds. They aren't just locations—they're emotional landmarks.

The setting also dictates rhythm. If your characters are in a dense jungle, movement is slow. Every sound matters. Paranoia builds. If they're in a desert, the heat becomes a constant threat. Silence stretches. Time feels strange. Snowy landscapes muffle gunshots. Urban settings echo them. The physicality of your environment influences not just the plot but the *pace* of the narrative. Use that. Let the setting shape the beats of your story like any other character would.

In stories where the enemy is distant or abstract, the setting often takes its place. A minefield can feel more threatening than a sniper. A collapsing building can feel more urgent than an advancing tank. When you let the environment play an active role, you tap into something visceral. It adds tension, unpredictability, and urgency. The weather changes a mission. The terrain separates the group. A missed path leads to disaster. The setting is never neutral—it's either with your characters or against them.

You can use contrast in setting to enhance emotion. A peaceful landscape during a brutal mission. A quiet snowfall after a massacre. A child's drawing on the wall of a ruined schoolhouse. These juxtapositions force your audience to see the war through emotional eyes. They highlight what's been lost. They give weight to what's at stake. When the setting reflects the inner conflict of your characters—or stands in stark opposition to it—it deepens the impact.

Don't forget that your characters carry the setting with them, even when they leave it. The soldier who returns home from war sees the world differently. A crowded street feels like a threat. Fireworks sound like incoming shells. Peace feels unreal. That sense of displacement is part of the setting too. It lives in the character's memory. The war never fully ends. It just shifts location—from the outside world into the mind.

ChatGPT can help you flesh out your war setting with sensory detail. Try prompts like, "Describe a war-torn city from the point of view of a nurse looking for survivors," or "Paint a picture of a trench at midnight in winter, from the perspective of a young soldier." Use the responses to get a feel for what your setting might *feel* like to your characters. Then take those details and ground them in your emotional tone. Let the setting evolve as your characters do. A ruined church at the start of the story might feel hopeless. By the end, it might feel sacred, even if it's still in ruins.

The setting can also carry its own arc. At the beginning of your story, the landscape might be whole, untouched. By the middle, it's scarred. By the end, it's a ghost of what it was. Let that visual transformation mirror the emotional journey of your characters. The destruction of the setting can parallel the loss of innocence, the collapse of ideals, or the fracturing of relationships. Or its quiet rebirth—a single flower blooming in the rubble—can hint at healing.

Your setting also speaks to the historical, political, and moral context of your story. A jungle in Vietnam doesn't just tell us where we are—it brings with it the entire emotional history of that war. A village on the Eastern Front during World War II carries different ghosts than a base in Afghanistan. Even fictional settings carry weight. A moon colony at war with Earth might be pure sci-fi, but you can design it to reflect real-world emotions—oppression, resistance, isolation, fear. When you treat your setting like a character, it becomes more than a map. It becomes a voice.

In the end, the war setting isn't just a place where things happen. It's a presence that breathes with your characters, bleeds with them, and changes with them. It's a reminder of what was, what is, and what might never be again. So treat it with the same care you give to your protagonist. Listen to it. Shape it with intention. Let it speak. Because when the war is over and your characters are counting the cost, the setting is the one thing that remains, holding the memory of everything that's been lost—and everything that still matters.

Building Tension from the First Scene

In a war drama, the first scene isn't just your introduction—it's your contract with the audience. You're telling them what kind of emotional terrain they're about to walk into. Are you about to break their heart? Grip their nerves? Leave them breathless, shocked, or quietly unnerved? The first scene sets the tone, the stakes, and the atmosphere—and if you do it right, it creates a pressure that doesn't let up, even in the quietest moments. Tension is your best friend in a war story. You don't need to wait for the first gunshot to make it show up. It can—and should—be there from the very first line.

The key to building tension early is to start with *questions, not answers.* Tension thrives on the unknown. Drop the reader or viewer into a world where something feels off, something is about to happen, or something terrible has already happened. Let them feel it before they understand it. A soldier alone in a silent forest. A radio crackling with static. A family packing in the dark, glancing toward the sky. A child waking up to find their parents missing. These are openings that lean into atmosphere, mystery, and anticipation. You don't need action to create suspense—you just need uncertainty.

Start small. The most effective first scenes don't always begin with a bang. They begin with something that makes us lean in. Think of a soldier cleaning their weapon while staring at a photograph. Think of a woman hiding a letter behind a loose brick as sirens wail in the distance. Think of a commander walking through a field of body bags in total silence. These images don't just introduce the setting—they introduce emotion, memory, fear. They tell us, without saying it, that war is already here, or that it's coming, and that everyone knows it.

Dialogue in your opening scene should carry weight without explanation. People under pressure don't talk in exposition. They hint, avoid, snap, whisper. A soldier saying, "We're not ready," is more effective than a paragraph explaining the enemy's advance. A mother telling her son, "Don't open the door for anyone—no matter what they say," is more haunting than a news report on the radio. Tension is built when the audience picks up on fear that isn't fully explained. When something's wrong but no one will name it.

One great technique is to introduce a *rhythm* that gets disrupted. Show normal life on the edge of collapse. Kids playing in the street, then scattering as planes roar overhead. A peaceful dinner interrupted by a knock at the door. A patrol making jokes until they find something they weren't supposed to. Establish a routine, a moment of human connection—and then cut it short. That contrast builds immediate tension because it shows how fragile peace is in a war zone.

Use sound. Even on the page, sound is powerful. The distant echo of artillery. The ticking of a watch. The buzz of a radio. The silence after a scream. These auditory cues set a mood. Readers feel what's happening before they see it. If you're writing a screenplay, your sound design begins here. If you're writing a novel, the way you describe sound will help your audience feel the tension in their bones. A sudden silence can be just as loud as an explosion.

You can also build tension through *time.* Put a clock on the scene. Something's coming. A decision has to be made. A deadline is looming. The convoy arrives in twenty minutes. The bombing starts at dawn. The border closes at midnight. When characters are racing against time, tension becomes baked into every line. Even if no one is running or shouting, the pressure is there. It raises questions. Will they make it? What happens if they don't? What are they willing to risk?

Another angle is to introduce *contradiction* right away. A soldier laughing while cleaning blood from their boots. A general crying in private before delivering orders. A child humming a lullaby in a city that's just been shelled. These contradictions create emotional dissonance, and that dissonance is a subtle form of tension. The audience knows something is wrong, even if they can't say why. That kind of unease draws them in, makes them pay attention. It makes the war feel personal before it ever turns violent.

Your opening scene should also introduce one clear emotion that will echo throughout the rest of the story. If the dominant emotion is fear, then let the first scene make us hold our breath. If it's grief, start with something already broken. If it's confusion, drop us into a moment where no one knows what to do. The emotion in that first scene becomes a thread that follows your characters through the entire war. It ties the first moment to the last.

You can use ChatGPT to generate a range of opening scenes. Try asking for a scene that starts with high tension but no violence, or a scene that begins quietly but hints at disaster. Explore variations. A soldier on a train, a nurse preparing supplies, a refugee crossing a border, a general reading an old letter. Each one can be shaped to hold a different kind of tension—internal, relational, or situational. Once you find a version that sticks with you, you'll know you've tapped into something emotionally true.

What you're doing in that first scene is building a door. The reader or viewer walks through it expecting answers, safety, maybe a hero. But what they find is fear, ambiguity, and decisions no one wants to make. And that's what makes war drama unforgettable. Tension doesn't mean nonstop action. It means emotional strain, moral pressure, the feeling that something vital is slipping through your fingers. When you build that from page one, the audience has no choice but to keep turning pages or watching the screen.

The first scene isn't about where the war starts. It's about where *your* war starts—the war inside your characters, the war in their memories, the war waiting just outside the door. And when the tension starts there, it follows them wherever they go. Through every skirmish. Every silence. Every goodbye. It becomes the invisible hand shaping everything they do. And that's what keeps your audience holding their breath, all the way to the end.

Writing the Calm before the Storm

There's a special kind of electricity in a war drama scene where nothing is happening—yet. No bullets are flying. No bombs are dropping. And still, the air is thick with dread. That's the calm before the storm, and when you write it well, it becomes one of the most powerful tools in your war drama arsenal. It's not just filler between action sequences. It's the space where your characters breathe, break, bond, or fall apart. It's where we see the truth of who they are when they know what's coming and can't do anything to stop it.

The calm before the storm doesn't mean everyone's actually calm. It means they're *waiting*. And waiting is its own kind of war. Soldiers fidgeting. Civilians whispering. A commander staring out into the dark, already running battle plans through their mind. This moment builds tension not through action but through *anticipation*. Everyone knows the storm is coming. They just don't know when or what form it will take. And that uncertainty is what makes the scene pulse with quiet, anxious energy.

This is where your characters' internal lives take center stage. When the guns are silent, people start thinking—about home, about death, about regrets, about love, about God, about what comes next. Some characters try to distract themselves. Others withdraw. Some crack jokes. Some say things they've been holding in for months. These pre-battle moments can be deeply human and often unforgettable. A soldier polishing his boots for no reason. A nurse humming an old song. A couple holding hands, knowing this might be their last night. These are the details that make the reader or viewer care about what happens when the storm finally hits.

It's also a moment where relationships deepen. When you're facing something terrifying, you cling to whatever comfort you can find. Maybe it's a fellow soldier. Maybe it's a photograph. Maybe it's a belief. Use this scene to explore character dynamics—alliances forming, tensions boiling over, secrets slipping out. A calm moment before battle might feature a shared smoke, a whispered argument, a confession. It's in this space that your characters become real. And when the shooting starts, those emotional threads will pay off in ways you can't get with action alone.

The physical environment plays a huge part in this kind of scene. Think about the sounds, the smells, the light. Rain tapping on a roof. The hum of distant engines. The smell of metal and sweat. A storm in nature can mirror the emotional one on the horizon. A quiet dawn can feel eerie instead of peaceful. The sky might look too still, the wind too gentle. When nature holds its breath, so does the reader. You can use that atmosphere to frame your characters' emotions and heighten the contrast between now and what's about to come.

Don't rush this scene. It's tempting to jump straight into the action, especially if the battle is already planned out in your head. But the power of the battle is rooted in how much we care when it begins. And that care is built right here. Give your characters a minute to reflect. Let the reader sit with the silence. Let the stillness stretch, because everyone knows it's temporary. That tension—emotional and narrative—will make the coming chaos hit even harder.

Use restraint in your dialogue. Let characters say only what they need to say—or say the wrong thing entirely. People don't always speak the truth when they're scared. Sometimes they hide behind jokes. Sometimes they pick fights over nothing. Sometimes they speak softly, because the silence is already screaming. Realistic, emotionally layered dialogue here can do more than exposition or foreshadowing ever could. A few well-chosen words between characters can carry more weight than a whole speech.

One of the most effective tools in this type of scene is *routine*. Showing characters engaging in mundane, repetitive tasks—cleaning weapons, writing letters, tightening boots, checking gear—adds to the tension. Because we know they're doing these things not out of peace, but out of habit, out of nerves, out of the need to cling to something normal. It creates contrast between what they're doing and what they're bracing for. That contradiction is emotionally rich and makes everything feel more fragile.

You can also use flashbacks or quiet monologues in these moments to deepen emotional resonance. A character remembering their childhood, or reliving a traumatic memory, can make this pause feel heavy rather than slow. You're giving the reader access to internal states that can't be accessed in the chaos of war. These reflective moments are where we learn what truly haunts your characters, what they're fighting for, and what they fear losing the most.

Ask ChatGPT to help generate these reflective or bonding scenes if you feel stuck. You can try prompts like, "A group of soldiers talking the night before a doomed mission," or "A nurse writing in her journal as bombing begins in the distance." Let the AI offer you a few emotional directions, and then take the one that rings truest for your characters. The goal isn't to show plot—it's to show heart.

The calm before the storm is also a powerful structural tool. It gives your audience time to breathe, time to feel, and time to anticipate. And when the storm finally comes—when the bullets rip through the quiet, when the sky lights up with fire—it means something. Not just because it's loud or dramatic, but because we've just seen the people who will live through it. Or won't. We've seen them as human beings, not just players on a battlefield.

In the end, writing the calm before the storm is about honoring the space between violence. It's about showing that silence can be louder than explosions. That stillness can hurt more than wounds. That time is never slower than in the minutes before everything changes. And when you give your characters the space to exist in that moment—not just as soldiers, or civilians, or symbols, but as people—you give your audience a reason to care when the storm finally breaks. And that's what turns a good war story into a great one.

Planning the Major War Events in Your Plot

When you're building the plot of a war drama, one of the biggest creative decisions you'll face is mapping out the major war events that will serve as the spine of your story. These are not just explosions or battles—they're emotional turning points, moments of irreversible change that shape the direction of your characters and the world they live in. Planning these events is like planning the seismic shifts in an earthquake. Each one reshapes the landscape, leaves a scar, and pushes your characters into new emotional and narrative territory.

The first thing to understand is that war events in a story are not just about physical conflict. They're about cause and consequence. A skirmish at the border isn't just gunfire—it might trigger a full invasion. The death of a leader isn't just tragic—it might create a power vacuum. A failed evacuation isn't just chaos—it might mean people are trapped. Every war event you plan needs to ripple outward and affect everything around it. If it doesn't change something for your characters, the story, or the world, then it's just noise.

A smart way to begin planning is by stepping back and asking, "What are the five or six big war moments that define this story?" These could be battles, bombings, missions, political shifts, betrayals, invasions, or uprisings. Think of them as tent-poles. You can build the story around them, knowing that each one needs to do something essential—it has to raise the stakes, shift the dynamics, deepen the emotional investment, or force your characters into new decisions.

Let's say your story begins with a small mission that goes sideways. That could be your first war event—a limited action with outsized consequences. It introduces the world, the danger, and maybe even hints that the leadership can't be trusted. Later, you might have a major turning point battle where a beloved character dies, fracturing the group. Then a retreat, where survival is the only goal. Then maybe an ambush or betrayal that changes who the enemy really is. And finally, the climactic event—one last stand, one desperate escape, one impossible choice. These events act as the map through your war story.

Each of these events should connect to your characters emotionally. That's the trick. You're not just showing history unfold—you're showing people being crushed, forged, or transformed by it. A battle that kills hundreds doesn't matter nearly as much as the one that leaves your protagonist holding a bloodied letter they never delivered. That's where the war becomes real—not in the numbers, but in the personal cost. Every event should be designed to affect someone deeply. The goal isn't just escalation—it's escalation with consequence.

You can use ChatGPT to help brainstorm these events. Feed in your story concept and ask, "What are five major war-related events that could shape this character's journey?" Or go broader—"Give me a timeline of fictional war events for a story set in a near-future civil war." You'll get structure ideas you can expand and personalize. If your story is inspired by real-world wars, you can ask for key events in similar conflicts, and then fictionalize or reframe them to suit your narrative.

Another useful approach is to think of war events in terms of emotional rhythm. Don't just pile up bigger and louder battles. Mix it up. A devastating loss followed by an uneasy peace. A sudden ambush after a moment of relief. A mission that seems like a success until it turns out to be a trap. This up-and-down motion keeps your story tense, unpredictable, and emotionally resonant. Readers and viewers aren't just waiting for the next bang—they're bracing for the next emotional blow.

War events don't have to be battles. One of the most chilling war scenes might be the discovery of an abandoned village. Or the arrival of a letter that never should have been opened. Or a broadcast announcing a ceasefire that no one believes.

These are major story events too. They don't need gunfire to shake the world. Sometimes the quietest moments are the most violent in terms of what they mean. Use that to your advantage.

Also think about geography. War isn't just about time—it's about space. Where do these events happen, and how does that shape the story? A mountain pass, a city in ruins, a jungle with no clear paths, a refugee convoy trying to cross a river under fire—each place changes the kind of conflict your characters will face. The terrain can be an ally or an enemy. Let each major war event unfold in a different kind of environment to keep the story visually and emotionally fresh.

Make room for unexpected consequences. A bombing that misses its target but hits a school. A spy who's discovered not by the enemy but by a frightened child. A radio message intercepted and misinterpreted. These moments inject realism and chaos into your war events, because war isn't clean, and plans rarely go the way they're supposed to. Let things go wrong, and then show how your characters react. That's where the human drama explodes.

Planning the major war events also gives you a framework for character arcs. Where is your protagonist emotionally before the first big battle? Who have they lost or found by the second event? What version of themselves do they become after the third? These events don't just shape the story—they shape your characters. Use them to break your characters open. That's where the truth of the war comes out.

Lastly, remember that your war drama doesn't end with the last battle. Think about what event follows the climax. What's the emotional aftermath? What does peace look like when it's stained with everything your characters endured? The final war event isn't a victory or defeat—it's a reckoning. The war may be over, but what your characters carry forward will shape the final image, the last line, the moment the audience walks away with.

Major war events aren't about spectacle. They're about transformation. Plan them with emotion. Deliver them with clarity. And let them ripple through the lives of your characters like shockwaves. Because in war, no one walks away unchanged—and neither should your audience.

Using ChatGPT to Outline Your Story Fast

One of the most overwhelming parts of writing a war drama is figuring out where to begin. You've got characters, you've got conflict, you've got ideas for emotional moments and dramatic turns—but shaping it all into a coherent structure? That's the part that can stall you for days. But here's the good news: you don't have to do it alone. With ChatGPT, you can outline your war story quickly, flexibly, and in a way that gets the creative fire burning instead of burning you out. When used right, it becomes your co-strategist—working alongside you to design the bones of your story before you dive into writing the flesh.

Start by having a clear sense of what kind of war story you want to tell. Is it a survival tale? A redemption arc? A story of resistance? A tragic fall? Once you know the emotional shape of your narrative, you can guide ChatGPT to create an outline that suits it. Try beginning with a prompt like, "Help me outline a war drama about a young soldier who becomes disillusioned with the military over the course of a doomed campaign." The clearer your initial premise, the better the outline that comes back to you.

If you don't know where to start, that's fine too. You can say something as simple as, "Give me a three-act structure for a war drama set during a fictional civil war," or "Create a rough outline for a story about a nurse in World War I who discovers a secret about a wounded officer." You'll get a basic skeleton—often with a beginning, middle, and end—that you can then tweak, reshape, and refine. It might not be perfect right away, but it will give you something to react to, which is often the most important thing in the early stages of planning.

Let's say ChatGPT returns with something like:

- **Act I**: Introduce the protagonist, the war-torn world, and the central moral dilemma. The character is hopeful, even patriotic.
- **Act II**: The protagonist faces loss, betrayal, and the horrifying reality of war. Loyalties are questioned, relationships are tested.
- **Act III**: A climactic moment forces a moral choice. The protagonist makes a sacrifice or commits to a new, painful truth.

That's a basic arc—but now you can take it and start filling in the details. Ask ChatGPT to expand Act I: "What events could happen in Act I that show the protagonist's innocence and set up the coming conflict?" You might get suggestions like witnessing an unfair execution, a naive letter home, or a moment of camaraderie with soldiers who won't survive Act II. You can follow up again: "How does the character begin to change in Act II? What events push them toward disillusionment?" Now you're building an emotional roadmap, with logic and resonance.

You can also use ChatGPT to generate plot points tailored to specific themes. If your war story is about grief, ask for scenes that reveal how your character processes death. If it's about guilt, ask for moments of failure and their emotional fallout. If it's about redemption, explore turning points that force the character to confront their past. ChatGPT won't always nail it on the first try, but it will give you a buffet of options you might not have come up with on your own.

Another helpful approach is using ChatGPT for character arcs that align with your outline. Once you've built the plot structure, you can ask, "How can each major event in the story affect the protagonist emotionally?" or "What does the supporting character learn at each stage of the war?" Now you're layering depth into your structure. You're making sure that your plot isn't just moving the story forward—it's evolving your characters.

And don't stop with just the hero. You can outline subplots too. Ask, "Give me a subplot for a cynical war photographer who sees too much and starts to care again." Or "What's a side story involving a civilian child who crosses paths with the soldiers?" Each one can be outlined in tandem with your main plot, giving you multiple threads to weave through your story and keeping it emotionally rich.

For stories with ensemble casts, you can outline separate threads and then ask ChatGPT to help you find intersections. "Where could the paths of these two characters cross in a meaningful way?" or "What shared event could unite this group?" You'll start to see the dramatic web forming—connections, conflicts, resolutions—all from a few well-phrased prompts.

If you want to go even faster, ask for a full scene breakdown. Say, "Give me a 10-scene outline for a war drama with a tragic ending," and you'll get a numbered list of narrative beats. You can ask for a version with fewer scenes or more, a lighter tone or a darker one, something intimate or something epic. Each version is a new lens, and you can merge elements from each to find the version that excites you most.

You can also reverse-engineer your story with ChatGPT. If you know how it ends—say your protagonist dies saving civilians—you can ask for a backward outline: "What events could lead up to this ending in a way that feels emotionally earned?" Working backwards is often the fastest way to outline a strong, structured narrative with a payoff that feels right.

The beauty of using ChatGPT to outline is that you can try 10 different versions without wasting days of effort. Each outline is a draft, a test, a dry run. You don't need to commit to any one version until it clicks. Let the AI do the heavy lifting so you can stay focused on the vision, the emotional resonance, the characters, the beats that make the story yours.

Outlining your war drama fast doesn't mean cutting corners. It means using tools to get out of your own way. Let ChatGPT help you bypass the pressure of the blank page. Let it show you paths you hadn't considered. Let it give you the first shape so you can bend, twist, break, and rebuild it into something personal, powerful, and unforgettable.

Because once the outline is in place, you're not guessing anymore. You're writing with direction. You know where you're going, who's going with you, and what it's all going to cost. And that's how your war story becomes more than just a series of events—it becomes an emotional journey from the first shot to the final silence.

Exploring the Hero's Journey in a War Context

The Hero's Journey is one of the most timeless storytelling frameworks we have, and when applied to a war drama, it doesn't just survive—it transforms. War adds weight, stakes, and moral complexity to every stage of the journey. It turns simple choices into life-or-death decisions and makes every transformation feel earned in blood, fire, and silence. The key is not to follow the Hero's Journey as a strict formula, but to use it as an emotional map. In war, the path is more dangerous, the lessons more brutal, and the cost of growth often devastating. But that's exactly why it works so well.

Let's start with the **Ordinary World**. In a war drama, the ordinary world isn't necessarily peaceful—it's just the world *before* the war shatters the character's sense of self. This could be a literal peacetime life: a farm boy dreaming of glory, a nurse treating common illnesses, a soldier training but never seeing real combat. Or it could be a world where the war is already raging, but the character has yet to face it personally. Either way, this is the moment to show who they are *before* the change. Innocent, eager, scared, stubborn—this is the baseline the audience will measure them against when everything begins to fall apart.

Then comes the **Call to Adventure**. In the context of war, this could be a draft notice, a bombing raid, a friend enlisting, an invasion, or even a personal loss that pushes the character to act. It doesn't have to be noble. It can be reluctant, fearful, even selfish. The important thing is that the character is pulled out of their normal world and thrust toward something much larger and far more dangerous. The audience should feel the shift. Something is happening now, and they can't go back.

Next is the **Refusal of the Call**, which is often where the emotional truth of your character starts to surface. They're not ready. They don't believe they can handle what's coming. Maybe they try to hide, run, or talk themselves out of it. Maybe they accept the mission, but their heart isn't in it. This is the moment where fear becomes visible. And in a war drama, fear isn't cowardice—it's humanity. Showing your character resist or question the call makes them relatable and layered, not weak.

The **Meeting with the Mentor** is especially powerful in a war story. This mentor doesn't have to be a wise old sage. It could be a grizzled sergeant, a field medic with too many scars, a cynical war photographer, or even a memory of a parent long gone. The mentor offers something essential—guidance, perspective, a weapon, a belief. They show the character a glimpse of what lies ahead, and perhaps how to survive it. And in war, mentors are rarely safe. They might die. They might fall from grace. They might become a symbol more than a person.

Crossing the **Threshold** in a war drama often means crossing into literal danger. The first battlefield. The first mission. The first time they see a body. There's no turning back. This is where the noise, the fear, and the disorientation kick in. The character isn't prepared, even if they think they are. And that vulnerability is what makes the moment so gripping. They're no longer a civilian or a trainee. They're in it now, and the war is real.

The **Tests, Allies, and Enemies** phase is where your character learns how war really works. They form bonds. They clash with others. They make mistakes. They see cruelty, bravery, beauty, and horror. Every battle, every loss, every act of kindness adds another layer. This is also where you can build your ensemble cast—each member reflecting a different response to war: anger, loyalty, fear, humor, numbness. Through these relationships, your hero grows—or cracks.

The **Approach to the Inmost Cave** is the lead-up to your story's emotional and physical climax. It's the most dangerous mission, the biggest risk, the darkest truth. Maybe it's a suicide run, a betrayal from within, a decision to abandon orders for something greater. This is where your protagonist faces the part of themselves they've been avoiding—the guilt, the doubt, the rage, the responsibility. It's not just about reaching an enemy stronghold. It's about reaching the edge of who they were.

The **Ordeal** is the storm. It's the moment everything breaks. Characters die. Plans fail. The protagonist is pushed to the edge. This might be the final battle, but it could also be something quieter but no less devastating—a moral choice, a failed rescue, a loss of faith. The ordeal is about transformation. Your character can't go back to who they were before. Not now. Something is lost. Something is learned. Something inside them has changed forever.

The Reward isn't always a victory. In war stories, the reward can be survival, understanding, or peace. It might be symbolic—a photo returned, a letter delivered, a grave marked. Maybe it's hope. Maybe it's simply the knowledge that they did the right thing, even if it cost them everything. What matters is that they've earned something through suffering, something no one can take from them.

The **Road Back** is often bitter. The war may not be over. The aftermath may be worse. The character begins the journey toward whatever world comes next, but they carry everything they've seen. Maybe they go home and can't sleep. Maybe they try to lead others. Maybe they walk away from it all. The road back is about consequences. The audience should feel the emotional weight pressing down with every step.

The **Resurrection** is the final test. One last moment that proves the character is not who they were before. They face a new challenge with a new sense of self. Maybe they find forgiveness. Maybe they save someone else. Maybe they lay down their weapon and refuse to keep killing. This is the hero reborn—not because they won, but because they survived with their soul intact.

And finally, **Return with the Elixir**. This isn't always literal. The "elixir" can be a new truth, a promise kept, a moment of connection. It's the thing your character brings home—or carries with them—that says, "This meant something." In a war drama, the ending isn't always happy. But it should feel *earned*. Even if the hero is gone, their journey should resonate. What they did, who they became, and what they gave up—that's the legacy. That's the story.

The Hero's Journey fits the war drama not because war creates heroes, but because it reveals them. It tests them. It tears them apart and dares them to become something more. Use the structure not as a checklist, but as a compass. Let it guide your character through the fire—and bring your audience with them, every harrowing step of the way.

Acts of Bravery, Betrayal, and Sacrifice

War drama lives and breathes in the extremes of human behavior. It's where ordinary people are forced to make impossible choices, where fear and duty wrestle for control, and where the worst and best of humanity reveal themselves—often in the same moment. Among the most emotionally explosive elements in any war story are acts of bravery, betrayal, and sacrifice. These moments become the emotional anchors of your narrative, and they can transform a character arc, change the course of the story, or define the tone of your entire drama.

Bravery in a war story isn't about being fearless. It's about pushing forward despite the fear. It's not always loud or cinematic. Sometimes it's quiet and deeply personal. A soldier shielding a friend from a blast. A civilian choosing to hide fugitives in their cellar. A medic crawling through rubble to reach a wounded child. These are moments of choice under pressure, and what makes them powerful is not just the action—but the *cost*. True bravery always comes with risk. If it doesn't, it's just confidence.

The most compelling acts of bravery are often unexpected. Maybe it comes from the least likely character—a timid recruit stepping forward when a veteran freezes. Maybe it's a character who's been selfish the entire story finally making the selfless move. These reversals hit hard because they challenge what we thought we knew. Bravery also doesn't have to be physical. Telling the truth in the face of danger, refusing an immoral order, admitting fear in front of others—these emotional risks carry just as much weight as charging into battle.

And then there's betrayal. If bravery is the ultimate test of loyalty, betrayal is the shattering of it. In a war drama, betrayal cuts deep because the stakes are life and death. Betrayal can be intentional—a spy selling out their squad. It can be cowardly—a character abandoning others to save themselves. Or it can be subtle—keeping a secret that dooms someone else. Whatever form it takes, betrayal creates immediate tension, emotional fallout, and lasting scars.

The most devastating betrayals are the ones that come from within the circle of trust. A best friend, a fellow soldier, a superior officer. Betrayal makes us question everything. Why did they do it? Were they always like this? Could it have been prevented? That emotional complexity keeps the audience hooked and your characters spinning. And betrayal doesn't always have to be evil. Sometimes it's done out of desperation, love, or survival. Those grey areas are where war drama shines brightest, because the audience is left to wrestle with the same questions the characters face.

Sacrifice is the most emotionally resonant of all. It's the choice to give up something—freedom, safety, a future, a life—for someone else. In a war drama, sacrifice doesn't always have to end in death. A character might stay behind to hold off the enemy, knowing they'll be captured. A mother might send her child away with strangers to keep them safe. A spy might expose themselves to save civilians. These acts strike at the heart of the story's theme: what are we willing to lose for something greater than ourselves?

The power of sacrifice is in its finality. The character doesn't come back from it. Their decision changes the story forever. And it should feel earned. A well-written sacrifice isn't about manipulating emotion—it's about delivering emotional truth. The best sacrifices echo throughout the rest of the story. Other characters carry that moment with them, haunted or inspired. The audience does too. And if the sacrifice ties directly to a character's arc—if it's the ultimate expression of how far they've come—it becomes unforgettable.

Use ChatGPT to explore these moments in advance. Ask, "Give me an unexpected act of bravery for a character who is normally selfish," or "Describe a betrayal that happens in a war camp and creates a moral crisis for the protagonist." You can also ask for ideas where all three—bravery, betrayal, and sacrifice—are tied together in a single sequence. That way, you're not just writing moments. You're crafting emotional explosions that reshape the entire landscape of your story.

These moments also give you a chance to slow down your pacing and really focus on emotional detail. What does the character feel *just before* they act? What do they think they're about to lose? Who's watching? What memory flashes through their mind? What's the last thing they say, if anything at all? You don't need pages of monologue—just a few honest, human beats can make the difference between a good moment and one that breaks your audience's heart.

Bravery, betrayal, and sacrifice also let you explore the moral territory of war. Who is the real hero? Who is the real villain? Can a betrayal be forgiven? Can a sacrifice feel wasted? In war, people don't always get what they deserve, and outcomes aren't always fair. But that doesn't mean they're meaningless. These are the moments that ask hard questions—and your audience wants to sit in those questions, even if they don't get an easy answer.

In many war dramas, these moments become the turning points. They shift the protagonist's belief system. They destroy relationships. They forge new alliances. Or they leave an empty space that can never be filled. If your story is an emotional battlefield, these are the explosions. Plan them carefully. Don't overuse them. Make each one count. When a character makes a choice that risks everything, that's when your war story becomes not just thrilling—but deeply human.

And maybe the most haunting thing about these acts is their silence. The soldier who dies alone after saving the squad. The letter that reveals a betrayal long after it's too late. The tearful goodbye that no one else sees. These are the ghosts your characters carry, long after the battle ends. And those ghosts? That's what your audience will remember most.

Choosing Your Story's Perspective and Voice

In the chaos and complexity of a war drama, one of the most important decisions you'll make as a writer is choosing your story's perspective and voice. This is how the audience will experience the war—through whose eyes, through what emotional filter, and with what level of insight. The battles, the losses, the betrayals, and the moments of bravery are all shaped by the lens you choose to tell them through. Get it right, and the story becomes intimate, urgent, and deeply human. Get it wrong, and even the most powerful scenes can feel distant or hollow.

Perspective is about point of view. Voice is about personality. Together, they shape everything your story says and how it says it. Let's start with perspective—do you want to tell your story in the first person, third person limited, third person omniscient, or something more experimental?

First person is incredibly personal. When a war story is told through "I," the reader lives inside that character's mind. They see what they see, feel what they feel, and hear their inner monologue during the quiet and the chaos. This perspective is powerful for emotionally charged war stories, especially those centered on trauma, guilt, or transformation. You can let the reader feel every tremor in the character's voice, every moment of hesitation, every haunting memory. But it also limits your scope. You only get what the character sees and knows. That can be claustrophobic—but in the right story, that's exactly what you want.

Third person limited gives you more flexibility while maintaining emotional intimacy. You're still close to one character—maybe your protagonist—but you're not stuck in their head. You can pull back a bit, describe what they don't notice, or give insight into how others perceive them. It's a great way to balance action and introspection. This perspective is especially effective in ensemble stories where you want to jump between different character threads while keeping the emotional tone grounded.

Then there's third person omniscient, where the narrator sees and knows everything. This voice can jump between characters, describe things no one in the story is aware of, and offer commentary. It's great for big, sweeping war stories where you want to show how the war affects many people, from soldiers to civilians to generals. But it can be hard to do well. If you're not careful, it can feel detached or overly authorial. It works best when you want the war itself to feel like a vast, uncontrollable force that touches everyone differently.

Some war stories even use second person, speaking directly to the reader as "you." It's rare, but in the right hands, it can be deeply immersive and unsettling. "You're running through the trees, heart pounding, smoke in your lungs." It pulls the reader into the experience of war in a visceral way. But it's tricky, and it works best for short stories or experimental fiction where the goal is to unsettle or provoke.

Once you've chosen a perspective, you have to figure out the voice—and this is where the story really comes alive. Voice isn't just what the narrator says—it's how they say it. It's the rhythm of the sentences, the kinds of words they use, the emotional tone that runs underneath. A war story told in a poetic, reflective voice will feel completely different than one told in a dry, blunt, soldier's cadence. Neither is wrong—but the voice needs to match the story you're telling.

If your protagonist is a hardened veteran, maybe their voice is rough, stripped of emotion, full of dry humor and hard-earned wisdom. If it's a young recruit, maybe the voice is full of nervous energy, wonder, confusion, and growing bitterness. If it's a nurse, the voice might be gentle, observant, emotionally burdened by what they witness day after day. Think of the voice as an extension of your character's emotional world. Let it reflect their history, their culture, their beliefs, their wounds.

You can also experiment with multiple voices if you're writing an ensemble piece. Let each character bring their own tone to the narrative. A war story told in alternating chapters—a soldier, a civilian, a journalist, a spy—each with a distinct voice, can give the reader a full, layered emotional experience of the war. But each voice must feel real and distinct. The dialogue, the descriptions, the way they interpret events—all of it should reflect *who* they are, not just *what* happens.

Voice can also help control the emotional tone of your story. A lyrical, almost dreamlike voice can turn the horrors of war into something surreal and haunting. A fragmented, staccato voice can reflect trauma or adrenaline. A dry, observational voice can create distance—sometimes useful in stories about desensitization or bureaucratic horror. And a voice full of anger, sarcasm, or despair can carry the reader deep into the character's moral struggle without spelling everything out.

Use ChatGPT to test different perspectives and voices quickly. Ask it to write a scene in first person, then rewrite the same scene in third person limited. Ask it to change the voice—make it poetic, then make it sarcastic, then make it clinical. You'll start to see how each version changes the emotional texture of the story. You might be surprised which version hits the hardest.

Remember, perspective and voice aren't just technical choices. They're emotional ones. They determine how close the reader gets to your characters, how the world feels, and what kind of emotional journey you're inviting your audience to take. A well-chosen voice can turn even a quiet scene into something unforgettable. A mismatched one can drain the power from even the most dramatic event.

So take your time with this decision. Try different angles. Let your characters speak, and really listen to how they sound. Once you find the voice that rings true, the story starts to flow. It feels right. And in a war drama, where every moment matters and every life counts, that voice is the one thing your reader will follow into the fire, into the silence, and into whatever comes next.

The Personal vs. the Political in War Stories

One of the most compelling dynamics in any war drama is the collision between the personal and the political. It's the space where individuals become trapped in the machinery of something much larger than themselves. Where a character's inner life—full of love, fear, loss, and hope—is constantly being shaped, distorted, or destroyed by decisions made far above their heads. When done right, this tension creates a war story that resonates on both an emotional and intellectual level. It's no longer just about who wins or loses the war—it's about what happens to the people caught in its gears.

At the heart of every war is politics. That doesn't mean your story needs to be about political leaders, laws, or ideology in an overt way. But it does mean that everything your characters go through—every mission, every displacement, every order, every betrayal—is touched by political motives. Someone made a choice to go to war. Someone decided who the enemy was. Someone signed off on that airstrike or that occupation. Your characters are living with the consequences of those choices, whether they agree with them or not.

But war stories are at their most powerful when they focus on the personal—on individuals trying to make sense of the world collapsing around them. A war nurse trying to save lives while politicians argue about borders. A young soldier drafted into a fight he doesn't believe in. A refugee family torn apart by policies they never voted for. These personal stories give the reader or viewer a way in. They take something massive and overwhelming and make it human-sized. You don't need to understand the entire geopolitical background of a war to feel something when a mother has to choose which child to carry across a checkpoint.

That said, ignoring the political altogether can make a war story feel hollow. You don't have to dive into complex diplomacy or deliver a history lecture—but hinting at the forces in play gives context to your characters' struggles. A soldier who begins to question the mission becomes more compelling when the mission itself is morally grey. A commander forced to carry out orders they don't believe in opens the door to explore the cost of obedience. Even small, passing details—a propaganda poster, a speech on a radio, a whispered rumor about corruption—can reveal the political undercurrents without slowing down the story.

You can use ChatGPT to help you build that political backdrop. Ask for summaries of real-world conflicts similar to your story's setting. Use that to shape fictional governments, alliances, rebellions, and power structures. Then ask, "How would these politics affect the people living in a border village?" or "What kind of laws would impact soldiers on the ground?" This way, you're not building a dry world—you're creating pressure that presses down on your characters from above.

Where this really gets interesting is when characters begin to clash—not over bullets, but over beliefs. One character might be loyal to their country no matter what. Another might see the whole war as a farce. One might fight for the cause, while another fights just to protect their family. When the political becomes personal, your characters are forced to face hard questions. Why are they fighting? Who are they fighting for? Are they doing the right thing—or just surviving?

And that's where war dramas have something truly powerful to offer. They give the audience a chance to see how ideology breaks down when blood is spilled. How simple slogans fall apart under the weight of grief. How loyalty and betrayal aren't always what they seem. When your characters are torn between personal values and political duty, your story starts to vibrate with emotional and philosophical tension. That's the stuff that lingers long after the credits roll or the final page is turned.

There's also space here for characters to become symbols without losing their humanity. A resistance fighter might represent freedom, but she's also tired, angry, and lonely. A defector might symbolize the collapse of a regime—but he's also someone who lost his brother in a bombing. Let your characters be individuals first. Let their choices be personal, even when they have political impact. That balance is what keeps the story grounded and emotionally rich.

One of the best ways to explore this dynamic is through contrast. Show two characters in the same situation, responding differently. A young recruit and a war-weary veteran. A political idealist and someone who's seen too much to believe in anything anymore. These character pairings allow you to dramatize the personal vs. political theme through dialogue, conflict, and change. They let you ask the big questions without ever needing a soapbox.

Tone is also key. If you take a subtle approach to politics, your story might feel more human and immediate. If you go in with a sharper, more analytical voice, you might pull back to show the larger system. Both approaches can work. It depends on the kind of war story you're telling. Is it about how individuals endure powerlessness, or how people fight to reclaim their agency? Is it about survival, or resistance? Or both?

And don't be afraid to show contradictions. A character might say they hate the war while continuing to fight. Another might claim to be apolitical, but make choices with huge political consequences. People are rarely consistent under extreme pressure. That inconsistency is human—and incredibly compelling.

In the end, the personal and political aren't two separate forces in a war drama. They're always intertwined. What your character believes influences how they act. What happens to them personally often reflects a much larger system at work. Let that interplay drive your story. Let it shape your conflicts, your character arcs, and your themes. Because when the gunfire stops, and the dust settles, it's not just the nation that's changed—it's the people who had to live through it. And those people, caught between loyalty and survival, grief and ideology, truth and silence—that's where your war story finds its deepest, most unforgettable power.

Pacing Your War Drama for Maximum Impact

Pacing a war drama is like conducting an orchestra. You're not just playing loud and fast all the time—that would wear out your audience in the first act. Instead, you're working with emotional highs and lows, the rhythm of action and reflection, the tension of anticipation and the release of consequence. When you get the pacing right, your story doesn't just move—it resonates. It pulls the audience forward with a heartbeat that mirrors your characters' inner lives. Every pause, every outburst, every quiet moment becomes intentional. And that's how you make a war story unforgettable.

Many writers feel pressure to keep the story moving with constant action. But war, in reality, isn't nonstop explosions and firefights. It's long stretches of waiting, tension, boredom, and fear punctuated by sudden moments of chaos and irreversible change. The pacing of your story should reflect that reality. If you run too hot for too long, your story loses impact. If you stay too quiet, your audience might drift. The art is in how you balance the two.

A well-paced war drama often begins with a slow build. You're establishing characters, the world, the emotional terrain. This is where you plant seeds—relationships, conflicts, routines—so that when the first major war event hits, it *means* something. Don't feel like you need to rush to the first gunshot. Let the quiet breathe. Let the audience settle in. If they care about the people before the war reaches them, they'll care even more when it does.

When the first major conflict arrives, shift the pace. Speed it up. Shorter sentences. Sharper dialogue. Snaps in emotion. Action scenes work best when the writing mirrors the experience. Quick cuts. Sensory overload. Confusion. Movement. But don't let it go on too long without grounding. After the action, you need a pause. That's where the emotional consequences hit. Who died? Who lived? What changed? That's where the audience feels the weight of what just happened.

Use this natural rise and fall to shape your structure. Think of your story in terms of emotional waves. Action leads to consequence. Consequence leads to reflection. Reflection leads to decision. Decision leads to new action. This pattern helps you build rhythm without losing tension. It also lets you explore your characters more deeply. What do they do after a mission fails? How do they react when they're alone with their thoughts? What choices do they make when they think no one is watching?

Silence is one of your most powerful tools. A silent moment after a bombing. A long look between characters who can't say what they feel. A still room where someone reads a letter they wish they never received. These quiet beats slow the pace intentionally—and they give your story gravity. Don't be afraid to hold on a scene. If it's emotionally charged, let it linger. Let the audience sit in the discomfort. Not everything needs to move at the speed of fear.

You can also use pacing to reflect your protagonist's inner arc. In the beginning, maybe they're eager, charging forward, full of energy. As the war wears on, their pace slows. They hesitate more. They second-guess. Or maybe it's the opposite—they start passive and afraid, and by the climax, they're moving fast, making bold choices, driven by desperation or purpose. Let the pacing of the story echo the emotional pacing of your main character. That way, the audience doesn't just *see* the change—they *feel* it.

If you're working with an ensemble, you can vary pacing by shifting perspective. One character might be deep in combat while another is trapped in a bunker with a radio and nothing to do but wait. Cut between those experiences to keep the audience engaged. Use contrast to create momentum. And always think about what each scene is *doing*—is it building tension, releasing it, complicating things, or clarifying something? Every scene should have a role in the pacing machine.

Midway through your story, the pace often dips—and that's okay. This is where you can focus on emotional weight. A sense of fatigue. Maybe even hopelessness. Use this as an intentional slowdown. It mirrors the exhaustion of war. But don't let it stall. Introduce a shift—a twist, a betrayal, a revelation—that launches the second half with renewed urgency. That's how you avoid the dreaded mid-story sag.

Toward the end, you'll naturally want to speed things up. The stakes are higher. The war is reaching a turning point. The characters are out of time. Your pacing here should reflect the urgency. But don't sprint the whole way to the end. Choose your moments. If everything is fast, then *nothing* feels fast. Save the real acceleration for the climax, when all the threads converge. And right after that, slow down again. Let the ending breathe. Let the audience feel the aftermath.

ChatGPT is a great tool for pacing support. You can ask it to generate beat sheets or scene outlines based on your current story draft. Ask it, "Where can I slow the pace for emotional weight?" or "What's a good moment to accelerate the tension?" Use it to test structural patterns—three-act, five-act, or even episodic models—to see how pacing naturally flows in different setups. Let it show you what happens when you rearrange events, or compress scenes, or insert flashbacks. Then tweak those ideas to fit your own rhythm.

Music is another way to think about pacing. Each scene has a tempo. An action scene might be a drumbeat, a conversation might be a violin, a tragedy might be a cello. When you score your scenes in your mind, you start to hear how the story moves. This is especially useful if you're writing for film or TV, but even in novels, it helps keep your storytelling instinct tuned to the emotional beat.

Pacing isn't about speed—it's about control. Knowing when to push, when to hold, when to stop. It's about guiding your audience through a rollercoaster that doesn't just thrill them, but *moves* them. A great war drama doesn't rush its moments, and it doesn't drag its action. It dances between them with purpose. So trust the rhythm of your story. Feel your way through the beats. And remember that the most powerful scenes aren't always the loudest—they're the ones that hit at exactly the right moment, with exactly the right weight.

Using Flashbacks and Memory in War Stories

Flashbacks and memory are not just tools in a war story—they're emotional minefields. When used well, they give your characters depth, haunt the present with the past, and let your audience understand what your characters have lost, what they're holding onto, and what they're trying to forget. War stories are often about survival, but they're just as much about remembrance. Even in the middle of the action, your characters are never fully in the moment. They're always carrying something from before—a face, a voice, a promise, a wound—and flashbacks are how you show that without slowing the story down.

A flashback isn't just a cutaway scene—it's a window into your character's soul. It reveals who they were before the war, what shaped them, and what emotional baggage they're dragging through every mission, every battle, every sleepless night. It's not just about backstory—it's about perspective. And when it's placed at the right time, a flashback can turn an ordinary moment into something devastating or poetic.

One of the best uses of flashbacks in war dramas is to create contrast. Show who the character used to be before the war hollowed them out. Maybe they were light-hearted, maybe they were in love, maybe they had faith in something. Then bring the audience back to the present, where that person is gone or changed. That emotional contrast adds weight. It reminds us that war doesn't just kill—it transforms.

You don't have to write full flashback scenes to make an impact. Sometimes a memory is just a fragment—a flash of a birthday, the smell of bread in a family kitchen, the sound of a song playing on a record before the invasion. These sensory cues can come in the middle of chaos. A soldier sees a burned-down church and suddenly remembers a Sunday morning with his mother. A nurse washes blood off her hands and remembers painting with her child. These moments don't interrupt the flow—they deepen it. They layer the action with meaning.

Flashbacks can also be triggered by emotional spikes. A near-death experience. A violent act. A quiet moment of stillness. Trauma doesn't operate on a schedule—it erupts. One minute your character is focused, the next they're swallowed by something they've been avoiding. This kind of psychological realism is powerful in war drama. It reminds the audience that what's happening now is only half the battle. The other half is happening inside.

But there's a fine line between using flashbacks for depth and using them as a crutch. You don't want to rely on flashbacks to explain everything. Don't use them to repeat information you've already hinted at. Instead, use them to reveal new dimensions of a character. Maybe they've been brave for most of the story, but a flashback reveals a moment of fear or failure. Maybe they've been cold, and the memory shows who they used to love. Flashbacks should surprise us emotionally—not just fill in blanks.

Structure-wise, you have a lot of freedom with how you deploy them. Some writers open their war stories with a flashback and return to it later, letting it slowly reveal the deeper truth. Others weave them in throughout, like emotional landmines that explode when least expected. You might use a recurring memory that changes meaning as the story progresses. Maybe a phrase someone said before the war takes on new weight after every loss. Or an image—a child's face, a field of sunflowers, a broken watch—that carries symbolic power.

You can also use flashbacks to connect characters. Two people from different sides of the conflict might both flash back to similar experiences—a childhood game, a family ritual, a schoolyard fight. This kind of parallel memory creates empathy without needing long speeches. It's a quiet way to say, "Even here, even now, we're not so different."

Flashbacks are also great for theme. If your war story is about loss, memory becomes a character of its own. What we remember, what we forget, what we distort to survive—all of it shapes how characters act and how audiences feel. Some characters might cling to memories like lifelines. Others might bury them deep. You can use flashbacks to explore how memory itself can be a form of resistance, or a form of denial, or even a weapon. A character haunted by a memory might make choices to avoid repeating it—or might be driven to seek revenge because of it.

ChatGPT is perfect for testing different memory scenes. You can ask it to create a flashback from a character's childhood that influences how they act in the present. Or you can generate variations—"Give me a memory that changes the meaning of a character's current actions," or "Write a quiet flashback that shows what the character has lost." Then take that raw material and fine-tune it until it fits seamlessly into your story.

Visually and tonally, flashbacks should feel different from the present. If you're writing for screen, the lighting, sound, and editing might shift. If you're writing prose, change the sentence rhythm, use different imagery, soften or sharpen the tone. Let the reader or viewer feel the transition. Let them know they've slipped into another layer of the story, and then guide them gently back.

And remember—not all memories are true. Flashbacks can be unreliable. A character might remember something the way they *want* to remember it. Later, you might show the real version—and that reversal can be emotionally devastating. The unreliability of memory adds depth and mystery, especially in stories where trauma or guilt are central themes.

Ultimately, flashbacks and memory give your war drama its soul. They remind us that war doesn't just happen in the present—it echoes backward and forward. It touches the innocent, the distant, the forgotten. It lives in the minds of those who carry on, sometimes more painfully than in those who didn't make it. When you use flashbacks with intention and restraint, you're not just telling your audience what happened. You're letting them *feel* what it meant—and in war stories, that's where the real truth lives.

Portraying Trauma and PTSD with Depth

In war dramas, trauma isn't just a subplot—it's often the quiet center of the story, pulsing behind every moment of action, every silence, and every choice a character makes. Portraying trauma and PTSD with honesty, respect, and emotional depth gives your war story gravity. It turns your characters from archetypes into real people. It reminds your audience that the war doesn't end when the fighting stops. And if done well, it can open hearts, start conversations, and leave a lasting impact long after the final page or scene.

The first thing to understand is that trauma looks different in everyone. There's no single way PTSD manifests. One character might break down during a quiet moment. Another might get colder, more controlled, more detached. One might lash out in anger, while another becomes fearful of everyday situations. Some carry their trauma silently for years before anything cracks. Others crumble quickly. What matters is that you don't reduce trauma to a cliché or a plot device. It's not about a soldier screaming in their sleep or flinching at fireworks—though those are real symptoms. It's about how the mind struggles to make sense of horror, and how that struggle bleeds into daily life.

PTSD, especially in the context of war, often shows up in fragments. It doesn't announce itself. It creeps in through nightmares, flashbacks, insomnia, hypervigilance, emotional numbness, or a short fuse. Characters might avoid people or places that remind them of the war. They might keep routines obsessively, trying to find control in a chaotic world. They might shut down emotionally—not because they don't feel, but because feeling too much is dangerous. These are the kinds of details that create authenticity.

Trauma also impacts relationships. Characters with PTSD may struggle to connect with loved ones. They might feel guilt for surviving. They might push people away to avoid being a burden. This isolation is powerful to show in your story. A protagonist returning home to a family that doesn't understand what they've seen. A medic who can save others but doesn't know how to heal herself. A soldier who can't stop reliving one moment of failure or loss. These dynamics create tension that goes beyond physical conflict—they bring war into the emotional and domestic space.

One of the most powerful ways to portray trauma is through behavior that *doesn't seem dramatic on the surface*. A character who won't sit with their back to the door. One who avoids silence. One who keeps a weapon nearby at all times, even when it makes no sense. A moment where they freeze instead of act. These subtle details show the lasting effects of trauma without needing to spell everything out. Let the audience feel the tension in the character's body, in their choices, in the spaces between their words.

Use memory and flashback carefully. A flashback should never feel like an excuse to show more battle footage or horror—it should feel like a loss of control. A character thinks they're fine, but then something triggers them. A smell. A sound. A phrase. Suddenly, they're *back there*, and the present slips away. That disorientation, that panic—it's not just for show. It's real. And when you portray it with restraint and emotional truth, it hits hard.

Shame and guilt are often companions to trauma. Survivors might question why they lived while others didn't. They might obsess over something they did or didn't do. They might feel like they can't ever be whole again. That internal conflict—between wanting to move on and feeling like they don't deserve to—is rich territory for storytelling. You don't need to solve it. Just let the audience sit in it, witness it, feel it.

PTSD isn't just about reliving trauma—it's also about the struggle to *re-enter life*. A war veteran trying to hold down a job, trying to be a parent, trying to laugh at things again. The disconnect between the war world and the civilian world can be overwhelming. Everyday problems might feel trivial, or strangely threatening. Writing scenes where your character has to navigate this contrast can be deeply moving. A crowd at a market might feel like an ambush. A family dinner might feel more emotionally exhausting than combat. These are the emotional beats where trauma becomes visible without being explained.

And while it's important to show the pain, it's also important to show resilience. PTSD is not the end of a person's story. Many people with trauma find ways to live, to love, to grow, to heal. That process isn't linear. There are setbacks, relapses, breakdowns. But there can also be breakthroughs. A moment of connection. A day without nightmares. A choice to seek help. If you choose to show healing, do it honestly—slowly, messily, without pretending everything is fixed. The goal isn't a clean ending. It's a believable one.

You can use ChatGPT to generate trauma-informed character arcs. Try prompts like, "Create a character who develops PTSD after a failed rescue mission," or "Show how a former soldier struggles with civilian life five years after the war." Let it help you explore the emotional terrain, then personalize it with your character's history, relationships, and beliefs. You can also ask for therapy dialogue, journal entries, or scenes where the trauma bubbles up in unexpected ways.

Talk to people. Read memoirs. Listen to interviews with veterans, nurses, survivors. Not just about what happened to them—but how it made them feel. What they remember. What they wish they could forget. The most truthful portrayals of trauma come from empathy, not imagination.

And remember, portraying PTSD with depth doesn't mean making your character broken. It means showing that they've been through something that changed them. That they're still fighting, in ways that might not look heroic—but absolutely are. Because surviving war is one kind of strength. Learning to live after it—that's another. And your story, if told with care and truth, might help someone feel seen. That's the real power of writing trauma with depth.

Capturing the Chaos of Combat

Writing a combat scene in a war drama isn't just about noise, bullets, and body counts—it's about *chaos*. It's about disorientation, fear, adrenaline, panic, confusion, and moments of impossible clarity in a storm of madness. When you capture combat effectively on the page or screen, you don't just describe a firefight. You make the audience *feel* it. You trap them in the moment with your characters. You speed up their heartbeat, tighten their chest, and blur their sense of direction—because that's what real combat does to people.

To start, forget the idea that combat is clean, choreographed, or cinematic. It isn't orderly. It isn't stylish. It's messy, fast, and often doesn't make sense until long after it's over. If your characters are confused, your audience should be too. That's not a flaw—that's authenticity. You're not trying to map out every movement like a chess game. You're showing what it's like to live inside the fight.

The most important thing to anchor your combat scene is *point of view*. Who are we with? What do they see, hear, feel? If you're writing from a close third person or first person, let that perspective shape everything. Maybe your character doesn't know where the shots are coming from. Maybe they lose track of their squad. Maybe they can't hear anything but ringing in their ears. Describe what they *notice*—not what the reader needs to know. Combat is sensory overload. Smoke, screams, radio static, mud in the eyes, the kick of the rifle, the sting of debris—all of it matters.

Pacing is everything. In action-heavy scenes, tighten your sentences. Make them fast, clipped, even abrupt. Long, flowing prose doesn't belong here unless it's intentional—unless it's showing how time slows down in a moment of panic or focus. You can use a sudden shift in tempo to reflect emotional spikes. A burst of short, sharp lines can mirror the rhythm of gunfire. A sudden pause—a single sentence stretching into stillness—can mirror shock, injury, or death.

And then there's confusion. One of the most realistic ways to portray combat is to let your characters *misunderstand* what's happening. A soldier might fire at shadows. A medic might run to help someone only to find they're already gone. A commander might give an order no one hears. A retreat might be mistaken for a charge. Let your audience feel that panic. Clarity should come later, in the quiet, when the smoke clears and the damage is counted. But during combat? Lean into the chaos.

Use contrast to make the scene more vivid. The sudden calm before an ambush. The quiet whimper of someone praying while artillery lands nearby. The sound of laughter turning to screams. These juxtapositions make combat scenes hit harder than nonstop violence ever could. Show the moment when the sun breaks through smoke. The absurdity of a bird flying through a battlefield. These details ground the action in human reality. They make it feel real because they feel *strange*, and war is full of strange moments that defy expectation.

Dialogue in combat should be minimal and functional. Yelling, orders, swearing, calls for help. There's no time for speeches. Keep it raw and short. "Cover me!" "I'm hit!" "Where's the sergeant?" "Go! Go! Go!" But also don't be afraid of silence. Sometimes there's nothing to say. A glance between characters. A scream that gets choked off. A hand reaching for help and not finding it. These are the emotional beats that make the action resonate.

You can also use combat scenes to reflect character arcs. Who freezes? Who pushes forward? Who becomes someone they don't recognize? The choices characters make in the heat of battle reveal who they are under pressure. A character who's hesitant to kill might be forced to act. Another might enjoy the violence more than they admit. A quiet soldier might take command when no one else can. These moments aren't just about surviving—they're about transformation.

Technology and weapons matter, but don't overdo it. Unless your story is specifically about military hardware, focus on how those tools affect your characters emotionally and physically. What does it *feel* like to fire a machine gun for the first time? What does a tank sound like when it's coming straight at you? What does an explosion do to your hearing, your vision, your sense of time? Use those moments to pull the audience deeper into the scene.

You can use ChatGPT to help build combat sequences by feeding in character details, setting, and emotional context. Ask for, "A combat scene where a young soldier experiences his first firefight and doesn't know where the shots are coming from," or "A battle that breaks out suddenly during a routine patrol." You'll get raw material you can reshape, emotional cues you can deepen, and pacing ideas that can help you control the flow of the scene.

And remember, not every combat scene has to be big. A gunfight in an alley. A sniper holding a street. A one-on-one struggle in the mud. These smaller-scale encounters can often feel more intense than giant battlefield sequences because they're personal. The stakes are immediate and direct. Use those moments to tighten the emotional lens and raise the tension.

Once the fight ends, don't rush away from the aftermath. That's where the real weight is. Who's still breathing? Who's missing? What did the characters lose—not just in bodies, but in themselves? Sometimes the real pain doesn't come from getting shot—it comes from looking someone in the eye and realizing you left them behind. Let the silence after combat stretch. Let it say everything the chaos couldn't.

Capturing the chaos of combat is about trust—trusting that the messiness of war doesn't need to be cleaned up for the story to work. In fact, the more disordered it feels, the more honest it becomes. Your job isn't to choreograph. It's to immerse. To trap the audience in a moment of pure survival, where choices are made in seconds, and everything changes in a heartbeat. That's what makes a combat scene unforgettable—not just the bullets, but the fear, the confusion, and the humanity that fights its way through the smoke.

Writing the War Room and Command Decisions

If the battlefield is where blood is spilled, then the war room is where the stakes are calculated. It's where lives are weighed, strategies debated, and the future is drafted in pencil and erased with bombs. Writing war room scenes is a chance to zoom out from the mud and chaos of the front lines and look at the minds steering the conflict from behind maps, screens, and closed doors. These scenes are not just about planning operations—they're about the moral weight of leadership, the politics of power, and the psychological toll of making choices that cost lives.

A war room can take many forms depending on the era and scope of your story. It might be a candle-lit tent with maps spread across a wooden table. It might be a bunker deep underground with blinking lights and radios. It might be a modern command center with digital displays and satellite feeds. What matters isn't the technology—it's the tension. The war room is not a place of comfort. It's a pressure cooker. And everyone inside it is either holding their ground, defending a decision, or fighting to be heard.

When you write these scenes, think about the people around that table. Generals. Strategists. Advisors. Politicians. Each has their own agenda, experience, and threshold for risk. Some may be cold and analytical. Others may be emotional, passionate, or out of their depth. This contrast creates drama even before a single move is made. The best war room scenes are arguments in disguise. Everyone's trying to steer the outcome, protect their interests, or follow their conscience. Sometimes they're fighting the enemy. Sometimes they're fighting each other.

Dialogue is crucial here. You want your war room scenes to crackle with urgency. Avoid speeches and long exposition. Let the tension live in clipped exchanges, interruptions, power plays. One character might be calm and composed, outlining a strategy. Another might explode with anger, pointing to casualties and failures. A third might try to mediate, but get drowned out. Let the scene feel like it could tip at any moment—not into violence, but into a terrible decision that will change the course of the war.

These are also scenes where your audience learns how strategy is shaped by more than just military logic. Maybe one side has superior numbers, but politics limits what they can do. Maybe a general wants to push forward, but the president needs a win for public morale. Maybe there's a supply shortage that changes everything. Let real-world complications interfere with clean, ideal plans. That's what makes it real. That's what raises the stakes.

You can use ChatGPT to draft these scenes quickly. Try prompts like, "A heated war room debate between a general and a civilian leader over a risky counter-offensive," or "A commander trying to justify a failed mission to their superiors." You'll get lines of dialogue, character dynamics, and ethical dilemmas you can tailor to your story. The goal is not just to show what decision gets made—but *how* it gets made, and what it costs the people in the room to make it.

A good trick to humanize these scenes is to anchor them in personal stakes. Maybe the general knows one of the squads they're sending in. Maybe someone around the table just got word that their own son was killed on the front. Maybe a decision will save one group but doom another. These tensions don't have to be spoken aloud. A pause. A glance. A character rubbing their temples before signing an order. These small emotional details speak volumes.

Another powerful element to include is doubt. No one should feel certain in a war room—at least, not the ones with humanity intact. Let your characters question themselves. Let them wrestle with the unknown. "Do we have enough intel?" "What if this is a trap?" "Are we doing the right thing?" These moments of hesitation don't slow down the story—they give it gravity. The audience should feel that every decision made in this room echoes outward, changing fates far beyond what anyone here can see.

You can also use the war room to create dramatic irony. The audience might know something the characters don't—a trap being laid, a betrayal in motion, a miscommunication that will cost lives. Watching leaders plan in the dark while the viewer knows the truth adds tension and dread, even in scenes where no weapons are fired.

Pacing is just as important here as it is on the battlefield. Build the scene like a ticking clock. Maybe there's a deadline. A missile launch window. An incoming attack. Each line of dialogue should push the tension higher. Then deliver a decision—and let that moment land. The silence after the call is made can be more powerful than any argument that came before it.

Once the decision is made, don't move on too quickly. Show the emotional aftermath. The weight. Maybe someone storms out. Maybe another sinks into a chair. Maybe a third character watches in silence, already doubting what they've agreed to. These human reactions remind your audience that behind every military manoeuvre are people who have to live with the consequences.

In war dramas, the war room isn't just the brain of the conflict—it's the heart under pressure. It's where the most agonizing truths get faced: that sometimes there is no good choice, that leaders are often forced to play God, and that even the smartest strategy can go terribly wrong. When you write these scenes with honesty and emotional weight, you show that war isn't just fought with guns and courage—it's fought with decisions that leave scars just as deep.

When War Becomes Survival

There's a moment in every war story where the objective shifts. It's no longer about winning. It's no longer about defending territory, following orders, or fighting for a cause. It becomes about *getting through the next hour*. Staying alive. Finding food. Avoiding bullets. Enduring pain. Holding onto something—anything—that still feels human. This is the point where war stops being a mission and becomes a raw, relentless struggle for survival. And when you write this transition with emotional depth, your story moves from dramatic to unforgettable.

Survival stories inside war dramas aren't just about physical endurance. They're about psychological collapse and moral pressure. They strip away everything your characters thought they believed in and expose what's left. Maybe it's instinct. Maybe it's memory. Maybe it's a promise made to someone they may never see again. Survival is primal, messy, intimate. It's not about who's the strongest—it's about who can adapt, who can endure, who can keep moving when everything is broken.

Often, this shift into survival mode comes after something traumatic. A failed mission. An ambush. A bombing. A betrayal. A retreat gone wrong. Your characters might be cut off, behind enemy lines, or left for dead. Their supplies are gone. Communication is lost. The chain of command has disintegrated. Now they're on their own. This is where things get quiet—and dangerous. Hunger, injury, weather, and fear become just as lethal as bullets. Your story slows down in some ways, but tightens in others. Every decision matters. Every mistake has consequences.

One way to make survival real is through sensory detail. This isn't the time for big sweeping panoramas. This is where you focus in close. The blistering heat or freezing cold. The gnawing hunger. The pain of a wound. The sound of something moving in the dark. The silence that feels like it's waiting to kill you. Show how your characters react. How they keep going—or don't. This is where the reader or viewer becomes fully immersed, feeling every breath, every heartbeat.

Survival also changes the rules. The soldier who used to follow orders may now have to break them. The medic who swore to protect life might be forced to kill. The character who once had faith might lose it. Or rediscover it in the strangest places. In survival, morals are tested. People do things they never thought they would—and sometimes hate themselves for it. Other times, they surprise even themselves with acts of courage or compassion. That's where the emotional power of survival storytelling lies: in the choices made when everything else has been stripped away.

You can also create compelling dynamics between characters during this stage. Maybe a small group is stranded together, and tension builds. One wants to push forward. One wants to surrender. One is losing their mind. The group starts to fracture. Secrets surface. Old wounds open. This microcosm of conflict mirrors the larger war but feels more personal. Every argument is sharper. Every bond is tested. Every decision splits them closer to life or death.

Don't forget about the psychological toll. Survival isn't just exhausting—it's destabilizing. People lose track of time. They hallucinate. They start talking to people who aren't there. They obsess over regrets. They break down when they realize they're not going home. Let your characters spiral a little. Let them confront the part of themselves they tried to bury. In survival, there's nowhere left to hide.

Use ChatGPT to explore these moments. Ask for a survival scene set in a snow-covered forest with two injured soldiers. Or generate dialogue between a group hiding in a basement, running out of food and hope. Try different emotional tones: despair, defiance, numbness, paranoia. Let the AI give you versions to experiment with—then refine them based on what feels most real for your characters.

The pacing of survival scenes should reflect the intensity of the situation. Some moments will crawl—long, drawn-out silences where nothing happens but everything feels dangerous. Others will explode without warning. A landmine. A sniper. A decision that backfires. That unpredictable rhythm is part of what makes survival so gripping. You want your audience on edge, never knowing what's coming next.

Also think about what survival *means* to your characters. Is it just about staying alive, or is there something bigger they're holding on for? A family? A promise? Revenge? Redemption? The goal can be anything, but it needs to be personal. When characters survive for a reason, their endurance feels earned. When they survive for nothing, it can be equally powerful—but infinitely more tragic. Either way, give their suffering meaning, even if that meaning shifts over time.

Survival changes people. By the time your characters make it out—if they do—they're not the same. And they shouldn't be. Show the toll. Show the cracks. Let survival mark them physically, mentally, emotionally. They might carry guilt. They might feel nothing at all. They might look fine but feel completely disconnected from the world around them. This dislocation is often where the most poignant part of the war drama lives—after the danger has passed, but the war inside continues.

In the end, writing war as survival is about narrowing your focus until the conflict becomes intensely personal. It's about finding truth in desperation. Humanity in horror. A heartbeat in the silence. These aren't just scenes of escape or endurance—they're the emotional core of your war drama. They're where your characters become more than soldiers, medics, refugees, or leaders. They become *survivors*. And in a war story, that might be the bravest, most devastating title of all.

Love and Loyalty amidst the Battlefield

Amid the horror and brutality of war, love and loyalty shine in ways that feel even more intense—because they exist in defiance of everything trying to destroy them. War has a way of stripping life down to the essentials, and when characters still find space for love, connection, and loyalty under fire, it speaks to something deeply human. These emotions become lifelines. They give your characters a reason to fight, to live, to hope. And when used with care, they add richness and emotional contrast to the grit and violence of your war drama.

Love in war stories comes in many forms. It can be romantic, platonic, familial, or even ideological. What makes it powerful is how fragile and urgent it becomes. In wartime, time is short, and the future is uncertain. A glance can say more than a speech. A kiss can carry the weight of a lifetime. A promise whispered before battle can mean everything. These moments don't have to be melodramatic—they just have to be *real*. Love, when placed in the middle of chaos, becomes the calm. The breath between explosions. The thing your characters hold onto when everything else is falling apart.

Romantic love during war is often rushed or unspoken. Characters don't always have time to explore feelings in depth. But that urgency creates intensity. A medic and a wounded soldier form a connection that might not survive the night. Two soldiers grow closer with every patrol, sharing cigarettes and stories they've never told anyone else. A civilian and a resistance fighter fall for each other, knowing it could end in betrayal or death. These relationships burn bright, because they *have to*. There's no guarantee of tomorrow. And that gives even the quietest moments a sharp emotional edge.

But love doesn't have to be romantic. Loyalty between comrades can be just as meaningful. The bond between soldiers who've watched each other bleed. The unspoken trust between a leader and their second-in-command. The connection between a refugee and the stranger who helps them survive. These relationships become the emotional foundation of your story. They're what make the losses feel real. When a loyal friend dies, it's not just another casualty. It's heartbreak. And when someone risks everything to protect someone they care about, it's not just heroism—it's love in its most selfless form.

Loyalty, especially in a war setting, is often complicated. Characters may be loyal to a cause, a country, a leader—or to each other. And those loyalties can conflict. A soldier might be torn between following orders and protecting a friend. A spy might be forced to choose between their mission and someone they've grown to care for. A civilian might betray their community to save their family. These are the emotional crossroads that elevate a war story. They force characters to reveal what matters most to them—and what they're willing to lose for it.

One of the most effective ways to explore love and loyalty in war is through contrast. Show moments of connection in the middle of destruction. A soldier finding an old letter in the ruins of a city. A nurse singing softly to a dying patient. A father and daughter separated by war but connected by a shared memory. These small, intimate moments can carry more emotional weight than an entire battle, because they remind the audience of what's at stake—not just lives, but hearts.

You can use ChatGPT to explore these dynamics quickly. Try prompts like, "Write a scene where two soldiers confess their love before a dangerous mission," or "Create a conflict between a commander and a soldier when loyalty to each other clashes with loyalty to their orders." You'll get dialogue, emotional cues, and potential arcs that can serve as inspiration or first drafts. Use them to discover angles you hadn't thought of. Let the AI help you dig deeper into how your characters relate to one another.

It's also powerful to show how love survives in absence. Letters that never get sent. Photographs kept in helmets. Memories that become a character's only comfort. These symbols of love—fragile, quiet, often invisible to others—are emotional anchors. They remind us that even in the most inhuman conditions, people still long to connect. Still long to matter to someone else. Still carry someone with them, even if only in thought.

But don't be afraid to show how war can twist love and loyalty too. Sometimes love becomes obsession. Sometimes loyalty becomes blind. A soldier might commit terrible acts out of devotion to a commanding officer. A character might stay loyal to a cause long after it's become corrupted. These arcs show the shadow side of these emotions. They remind us that love, while beautiful, isn't always pure. And loyalty, while noble, can sometimes be misplaced.

In the end, love and loyalty in a war drama don't need to be the center of the plot—but they should always be part of the emotional landscape. They're what make your characters feel human. They're what give the story heart. And they're what give the audience something to hope for, even when all seems lost.

When the bullets stop flying, and the smoke clears, it's not the strategies or the body count that people remember. It's the person who risked everything to save a friend. The couple who found a moment of peace in the middle of hell. The child who clung to a parent's words. The soldier who carried a letter in their pocket until the very end. These are the quiet explosions of emotion that live between the action scenes. And in those moments, your war drama finds its soul.

Civilian Resistance and Occupation Stories

Not every war story takes place on the battlefield. Some of the most powerful war dramas unfold quietly in alleyways, kitchens, schoolhouses, and underground tunnels—places where civilians live under the weight of occupation and choose, day by day, whether to submit, survive, or resist. These stories are often more intimate, more morally complex, and more emotionally charged than traditional combat narratives. They show what happens when war moves into people's homes, when oppression becomes routine, and when bravery takes the form of stolen food, secret meetings, or the risk of saying the wrong name at the wrong time.

Occupation stories are about imbalance. One group controls the streets, the food, the laws. The other group—the civilians—must learn how to navigate this new world, where danger is everywhere, and freedom is no longer a given. Some blend in. Some flee. Some resist. This constant pressure reshapes relationships, identities, and entire communities. Families are torn apart not just by bombs, but by choices. Neighbors spy on neighbors. Strangers become allies. The smallest act of defiance can lead to torture or death.

Writing these stories requires a shift in focus. You're not tracking troop movements—you're watching how power is enforced, and how people respond to it. The tension is often psychological and social. A mother hiding a radio under the floorboards. A child delivering secret messages. A priest offering sanctuary to hunted men. The stakes are deeply personal, and the consequences are brutal. The question at the heart of these stories isn't "Who wins the war?" but "Who do you become when your world is taken from you?"

One of the most compelling aspects of resistance stories is how ordinary people step into extraordinary roles. A shopkeeper becomes a code smuggler. A teacher distributes banned pamphlets. A teenager joins a sabotage ring. These transformations are emotional as well as practical. People must weigh the value of resistance against the risk to their families. And often, it's not black and white. Collaborators may have noble reasons. Resisters may make mistakes that cost innocent lives. That moral complexity is what makes these stories feel real.

You can use ChatGPT to explore different kinds of resistance movements. Ask for examples of civilian resistance in historical conflicts—World War II, Vietnam, Bosnia, or fictional dystopias—and then develop characters inspired by those realities. You can prompt the AI with, "Create a story about a resistance group operating under occupation in a small town," or "Describe how a baker uses their shop as a front for resistance activity." These details give you a foundation for building scenes that are full of tension and hidden danger.

Resistance doesn't always look heroic. Sometimes it's petty vandalism. Sometimes it's telling a lie that protects someone. Sometimes it's just *refusing* to give in. A woman continuing to teach her language in secret. A teenager writing graffiti messages after curfew. These small acts add up. They're not always recognized, but they show that even in the darkest times, people still try to hold on to dignity, culture, and hope.

But occupation stories don't just focus on the heroes. They should also show the collaborators—the people who enforce the occupation, or benefit from it. Some do it out of fear. Others out of greed. Some convince themselves they're helping. Maybe they're protecting their families. Maybe they believe the resistance is dangerous. Writing these characters with nuance is important. It makes the world feel lived-in, and it challenges the reader to question their own assumptions about what they would do under pressure.

One powerful angle is showing how relationships shift under occupation. Lovers turn on each other. Friends drift apart. A brother joins the resistance while a sister works with the occupiers. Secrets tear families in half. These deeply emotional fractures reflect the larger chaos of war and give your story its core tension. People don't just fight armies—they fight fear, silence, shame, and betrayal.

Setting plays a huge role in these stories. Occupied cities are full of contrast—military checkpoints next to bakeries, curfews enforced by patrols marching past lovers' apartments. Every familiar place becomes dangerous. Every corner could be watched. You can describe these settings with a heightened sense of awareness—how people look over their shoulders, how the city sounds at night, how language itself becomes coded. These environmental details put your audience in the skin of your characters.

Use pacing to create suspense. Occupation stories work well with slow burns. Long stretches of tension interrupted by sudden violence. A raid. An arrest. A secret discovered. Let the reader or viewer feel the dread building. Let them sit in the anxiety of what *might* happen. That way, when something does, it hits hard. The most gripping resistance stories aren't nonstop action—they're built on fear, patience, and the courage to act anyway.

Also explore the aftermath of resistance. Not every act succeeds. Not every resister survives. And even those who do may carry guilt, trauma, or a lifetime of consequences. What happens when the war ends, but the scars remain? What happens to the people who collaborated? What about the children raised in hiding? These are questions worth sitting with. The end of the occupation doesn't mean the end of the story—it just opens a new chapter, one that's often full of silence and reckoning.

Ultimately, stories about civilian resistance and occupation are about the power of choice. Who resists. Who conforms. Who watches. Who remembers. They show us that bravery doesn't always look like heroism. Sometimes it looks like surviving with your soul intact. Sometimes it looks like risking everything for one small act of truth.

And in those moments—when a father shields his daughter from soldiers, when a teenager lights a candle in defiance, when a community sings a forbidden song—you'll find the emotional heart of your war drama. These are the quiet, dangerous, unforgettable beats that remind us why we fight, why we endure, and why stories about war must also be stories about resistance.

The Role of Spies, Informants, and Double Agents

No war story is complete without the shadow war—the one waged not with bullets and bombs, but with whispers, secrets, coded messages, and betrayal. While soldiers fight on the battlefield, spies and informants move silently through the cracks, shaping the conflict in unseen ways. These characters—often misunderstood, mistrusted, or underestimated—carry enormous weight in a war drama. They are the manipulators, the observers, the survivors, and sometimes, the most emotionally fractured figures in your entire story. Writing them well adds a whole new layer of tension, deception, and moral ambiguity that transforms your narrative into something far more gripping.

Spies in war dramas are not James Bond-style action figures. They're not invincible, and they don't always get away clean. Often, they are ordinary people drawn into extraordinary roles because they had no choice. A resistance fighter pretending to work with the enemy. A translator who feeds intel to both sides. A clerk with access to classified documents who decides to act. These characters exist in the shadows between right and wrong, constantly balancing their mission against their fear of exposure. They lie to survive. They lie to serve. And sometimes, they lie to themselves.

The emotional tension of these roles is enormous. Imagine waking up every day knowing one wrong word, one wrong gesture, one misstep could get you killed—not in a blaze of glory, but in a basement, alone, tortured, forgotten. This tension is where your story comes alive. Spies don't just carry secrets—they *become* secrets. They live double lives, hide their true selves, and are often forced to betray people they care about. Writing their inner world is just as important as writing the covert missions. Show the cracks. The guilt. The constant calculation. The loneliness.

Informants are just as important, but often more tragic. They aren't full-time agents. They're often civilians, coerced into passing information—sometimes for money, sometimes under threat, sometimes out of ideology. They might inform on their neighbors, co-workers, friends. The power in writing informants lies in the emotional contradiction. They might hate what they're doing. Or they might believe they're doing the right thing. Either way, the consequences ripple outward. One tip-off can lead to a massacre. One withheld detail can change the course of a battle. These seemingly small choices have enormous weight, and your story can explore how those moments play out long after the report is filed.

Then come the double agents—the ultimate trust breakers. These characters are riddled with complexity. Are they loyal to one side but pretending to serve the other? Are they genuinely torn? Are they manipulating everyone? Or are they just trying to survive in a war where no side deserves their loyalty? Double agents allow you to explore betrayal in its most emotionally explosive form. A character who feeds intel to the enemy while sharing a bed with someone on their own side. A friend who turns out to have been watching your protagonist from the start. A leader who has been playing both ends against the middle. These reveals can shatter alliances, turn entire arcs upside down, and force your audience to question everything they've seen so far.

You can use ChatGPT to develop layered characters in these roles. Ask for a spy with a hidden motivation, or an informant who regrets every report they've made. Try prompts like, "Create a double agent who falls in love with someone on the side they're betraying," or "Write a scene where a resistance leader discovers the identity of a mole in their inner circle." These moments are charged, dangerous, and perfect for exploring themes of trust, identity, and deception.

When writing scenes involving spies, informants, or double agents, subtlety is your best tool. Dialogue is rarely direct. People speak in code, with meaning beneath every sentence. Facial expressions, body language, and timing matter more than exposition. A glance can be a warning. A silence can speak volumes. These characters live in the subtext, and so should their scenes. Let the audience lean in, trying to figure out who knows what, who's lying, who's playing who.

Also think about how these shadow figures affect your main characters. Maybe the protagonist relies on intel from someone they trust—only to discover too late that it was a trap. Maybe a side character's betrayal leads to a devastating loss. Maybe someone who's been quiet all along suddenly becomes the key to stopping a catastrophe. These characters don't need to be in every scene to have impact. One good spy can change the whole story.

And don't forget the stakes. The risk of being exposed should always be close. Let your spy sweat. Let them scramble. Let them make mistakes. There's more drama in a desperate cover-up than a clean escape. You can build entire chapters around a secret message almost being discovered, or a character trying to keep two identities from colliding. The best spy stories are less about gadgets and more about nerves.

Spies, informants, and double agents also give you a chance to explore the moral ambiguity of war. No one is pure in this world. Even the most noble cause requires lies. Even the most loyal soldier may be betrayed. Through these characters, you can ask hard questions: What is loyalty worth? When is it right to betray? Who decides who the enemy is?

In the end, these roles show us that war isn't just fought in trenches or skies—it's fought in whispers, locked doors, and glances across crowded rooms. It's fought by people who carry nothing but the truth and the risk of revealing it. And when you write them with depth, conflict, and emotional weight, these characters won't just surprise your readers—they'll haunt them. Because in war, the most dangerous weapon isn't a gun. It's the person you thought you could trust.

Exploring Moral Dilemmas in War

If war is chaos, then moral dilemmas are the anchor points where characters—and the audience—must stop and ask: *What is right?* War drama becomes truly gripping when the violence, strategy, and survival are interrupted by impossible questions. These are moments where your characters face choices that test the very core of who they are. No clear good or evil, no clean answers—just pressure, consequence, and the awareness that whatever choice they make, someone is going to suffer.

War doesn't just create external conflict—it throws internal conflict into overdrive. You can't tell a story about war without diving into the moral gray zones that come with it. These dilemmas aren't just plot points. They're emotional landmines. A soldier is ordered to fire on a building with civilians inside. A medic has to choose which wounded soldier to treat first, knowing the other will die. A spy must betray someone they love to save many. These decisions are agonizing not because they're complex on paper, but because they leave permanent scars on your characters' minds and souls.

The power in these dilemmas lies in how *personal* they are. The war may be political or ideological, but the moral crisis has to hit close to home. The audience needs to feel what the character is giving up—or giving in to. It's not just about choosing between two outcomes. It's about choosing who you are in the middle of the worst circumstances imaginable.

Often, the most compelling moral dilemmas come from characters trying to hold on to their humanity while surrounded by dehumanizing forces. A soldier who refuses to torture a prisoner, even if it might save lives. A resistance fighter who questions whether sabotage is worth the cost when civilians are caught in the blast. A commander who has to send a unit on a suicide mission to hold a critical line. These aren't about dramatic flair—they're about internal collapse and the cost of conscience.

You can build these dilemmas into your plot deliberately or let them surface organically as the characters face escalating pressure. Either way, you can use ChatGPT to help you brainstorm these scenarios. Ask for "moral dilemmas faced by medics in combat zones," or "a moment where a soldier must choose between following orders and doing what's right." You'll get the raw shape of the problem, and then you can refine it until it suits the emotional and narrative stakes of your story.

What makes these moments resonate is that there's no easy way out. Whichever choice the character makes, something is lost. And sometimes, they'll make the *wrong* choice. That's part of war, too. People act out of fear, pride, guilt, love, or desperation. They don't always do the noble thing. They do what they can live with—or what they think they can live with—only to find later that the burden is too much.

These are the moments that deepen your characters. After the action ends, after the gunfire fades, they're left with the weight of what they did—or didn't do. Maybe they try to justify it. Maybe they spiral. Maybe they shut down. Or maybe they find a way to keep going, carrying the choice like a wound. Moral dilemmas aren't just about the moment—they're about the *aftermath*. What changes in the character? What's broken? What won't heal?

You can also use moral dilemmas to spark conflict between characters. A squad might fracture after a decision made in the field. A commander might lose the respect of their unit. A soldier might turn on a friend who did something they can't forgive. These rifts add emotional tension and mirror the larger theme that war doesn't just destroy bodies—it destroys trust, certainty, and sometimes even hope.

Another layer to explore is how the moral line shifts over time. At the start of the war, your protagonist might have a clear sense of what's right and wrong. But the deeper they go, the more blurred it becomes. They may start justifying actions they once condemned. They may stop recognizing themselves. Or they may become even more rigid, holding onto their principles as a form of survival, even when it isolates them from others. Watching that transformation—or unraveling—adds tremendous emotional depth to your war drama.

You can frame these dilemmas around specific themes. Is your story about redemption? Then a character might be given a chance to make up for a past decision but at great cost. Is it about loyalty? Then a character may have to betray a friend to serve the greater good. Is it about survival? Then maybe the question becomes: How much humanity can you lose and still live with yourself?

It's also worth showing how moral dilemmas affect not just the person making the decision, but everyone around them. A wrong choice can lead to distrust, retaliation, or a ripple effect that changes the course of the war. These aren't isolated moments—they're fractures that spread outward, changing everything they touch.

And don't be afraid to revisit these choices. A character might think they made peace with something, only for it to come back in a dream, a letter, a confrontation. That's the truth of war—its ghosts don't just haunt the battlefield. They follow people home. They live in memory, in silence, in shame. They turn into the kinds of questions that don't go away.

In the end, moral dilemmas are where war stories find their deepest truths. Not in explosions or speeches, but in the moments when a character looks at two paths and knows that neither will leave them whole. These are the choices that define who your characters really are, and what kind of story you're telling. And for your audience, these are the moments that linger—the ones they replay in their minds, wondering what they would have done.

Because war isn't just about sides. It's about people caught in impossible situations, trying to do the right thing when right and wrong have both stopped making sense. And when you write that with honesty and emotional weight, your war drama becomes something more than just a story—it becomes a reflection of the human soul under fire.

The Power of Small Moments in Big Wars

In every sprawling war drama filled with explosions, troop movements, and sweeping battlescapes, it's often the quiet, intimate moments that leave the deepest mark. A war story isn't just about the big picture. It's also about the tiny moments that live in the spaces between orders and gunfire. A soldier tying a worn shoelace before heading into a firefight. A nurse whispering a lullaby to a wounded stranger. A shared meal, a glance, a joke told in the middle of hell. These fragments of humanity are what give war its meaning in storytelling. They anchor your audience in something real. Something human. Something unforgettable.

Big wars flatten people. They erase names and reduce thousands to statistics. But your job as a writer is to reverse that process. To reintroduce individuality. To slow the story down just long enough for the reader or viewer to feel something that can't be found in a report or history book. These small moments create contrast. When a character stops to light a cigarette, patch up a photo, write a letter, or brush the mud from their boots, we see the person underneath the uniform. And suddenly, the war feels heavier—because now we care about who might not make it through the next scene.

You don't need elaborate dialogue or lengthy description to make these moments land. In fact, restraint often makes them more powerful. A soldier watching birds fly overhead before a raid. A resistance fighter pausing to listen to music leaking from a hidden radio. A child staring at the stars through a shattered window. These images speak volumes, especially when juxtaposed against the noise and violence surrounding them. They remind us that beauty and pain can coexist. That people still seek meaning even when the world is falling apart.

You can use small moments to reveal character more effectively than an entire monologue. A man who always prays before battle, even though he says he doesn't believe. A woman who gives away her last piece of bread. A teenage scout who keeps drawing cartoons in his notebook despite everything. These choices tell us who they are. Not through what they say, but what they *do* when no one is looking.

Emotionally, these beats serve as pressure valves. War dramas are intense by nature, but relentless intensity can numb an audience. Small moments allow them to breathe—to reflect, to connect, to reset. They also build suspense in an unexpected way. A quiet moment often feels like the calm before a storm. The stillness makes the next explosion feel even louder. The silence sharpens the tension.

ChatGPT can help generate small, powerful moments by combining environment, emotion, and situation. Try prompts like, "Describe a quiet moment between two soldiers before a night attack," or "Write a scene where a nurse has a short, wordless interaction with a dying patient." Use these to build emotional depth in your characters without adding pages of backstory. You don't need to explain everything—just let a gesture, a detail, or a habit say what words can't.

These moments can also show transformation. The character who once rushed into danger now hesitates just long enough to pick up a fallen friend's dog tag. The soldier who hated poetry keeps a book of it tucked inside their coat. The civilian who vowed never to fight takes a deep breath and arms themselves for the first time. These small actions are turning points. They may not be highlighted with fanfare, but they change the character's course—and the reader will feel it.

Symbolism often lives in these moments, too. A child handing a soldier a flower. A soldier collecting keepsakes from each battle. A wedding ring held tight during interrogation. These objects and gestures carry meaning beyond their size. They become emotional anchors. Let them reappear throughout your story. Let the audience recognize their weight.

You can also use these moments to explore themes. If your war story is about memory, have a character obsessively write in a journal. If it's about sacrifice, show a character quietly giving away their rations. If it's about hope, give us a scene where someone plants a seed, fixes a toy, or hums a lullaby. Themes become real when they're grounded in action—not abstract ideas, but lived choices.

Tone is everything when crafting these beats. Let the language reflect the moment. Keep it simple. Don't overwrite. A few words can be enough when they're placed just right. A pause. A breath. A glance. These are the silences that speak. Don't rush them. Let them sit.

And remember that your audience is looking for *themselves* in these characters. They may not understand military strategy or political context, but they understand love, fear, loss, and laughter. A shared piece of chocolate in a foxhole. A half-finished letter tucked away. A soldier dancing alone to music only they can hear. These moments don't just humanize the story—they *universalize* it. They make the war feel close, no matter when or where it's set.

In the end, it's these small, human beats that your readers and viewers will carry with them. Not just the battles, but the people who lived between them. The man who never removed his lucky scarf. The woman who waited at the same place every day for news that never came. The soldier who found a kitten in a ruined building and kept it hidden in his coat. These aren't just side details. They're the soul of the story. And in a war drama, that soul is everything.

Because war, for all its scale and devastation, is lived one moment at a time. And the smallest ones often carry the most truth.

Writing the Turning Point of the War

Every war story eventually reaches that moment when the tide begins to shift—the point where what once felt inevitable suddenly becomes uncertain. The turning point of a war doesn't always announce itself with a massive victory or explosive defeat. Sometimes it's quiet. Sometimes it's a realization, a betrayal, a moment where morale breaks or surges. But whenever and however it comes, the turning point is where everything starts to change. And writing it well is one of the most satisfying and emotionally rich tasks in a war drama.

What makes a turning point powerful isn't just the shift in strategy or circumstance—it's the emotional effect it has on the characters and, by extension, the audience. The turning point should feel like a culmination of everything your characters have endured so far. It's not just a change in fortune—it's a change in tone, in hope, in belief. And often, it's the moment when your characters must reexamine their purpose and redefine what winning—or even surviving—actually means.

Before you write this moment, take time to build up the stakes. A turning point only works if the path before it felt inevitable. If your characters have been losing ground, barely holding on, or stuck in a hopeless situation, then the shift—no matter how small—will land like a thunderclap. Conversely, if they've been dominating the conflict, the turning point might come as a catastrophic mistake, a reversal that shakes their confidence and fractures their unity. Either way, the story should feel like it was headed in one direction... until suddenly it's not.

Turning points can take many forms. It might be a major battle that redefines the strategic landscape. It might be the death of a leader or the arrival of unexpected reinforcements. It might be the discovery of a traitor or a secret weapon. Or it might be something personal—a letter that changes a soldier's mind, a civilian uprising that shocks the occupiers, a small act of defiance that inspires a larger movement. The scale doesn't matter as much as the *impact*. This is the moment your characters—and your audience—realize the war is not going to play out the way they thought.

Think carefully about whose perspective you show this moment through. It doesn't always have to be your protagonist. Sometimes, showing the shift through the eyes of a secondary character adds more emotional weight. Imagine a soldier at the front hearing distant cheers and realizing the enemy is retreating. Or a young scout who stumbles on a supply convoy and realizes help is coming. Or a general looking at a map and realizing they've made a fatal miscalculation. These different points of view can add texture to the turning point and make it feel larger than any single character.

Use pacing and tone to underscore the shift. Before the turning point, everything should feel tight, heavy, and inevitable. Afterward, things should feel uncertain—maybe hopeful, maybe more dangerous. A good turning point doesn't just release tension; it replaces it with *different* tension. If things are starting to improve for your characters, the question becomes: Can they hold onto that advantage? Will the cost of this progress be too great? If things are falling apart, the question becomes: Who will survive this collapse? What will they lose along the way?

You can use ChatGPT to sketch out different versions of your turning point. Try asking for, "A turning point in a war story where the underdog army finally wins a small but symbolic battle," or "A scene where the discovery of a spy changes the tide of war." Play with variations. What if the turning point is misunderstood at first? What if it comes at the worst possible emotional time? What if the victory reveals a deeper loss? These complications make your turning point feel earned rather than convenient.

Symbolism can also enhance this moment. Maybe the rain finally stops. Maybe the enemy's flag is lowered for the first time. Maybe a long-absent sound—laughter, birdsong, music—returns. These small touches can add depth and signal to the audience that something fundamental has shifted. You're not just changing the trajectory of the plot—you're changing the emotional weather of the entire story.

And don't forget the cost. Turning points are never clean. Even if your characters gain ground, they've likely lost something to get there. A comrade. A belief. A piece of themselves. That duality—the mix of victory and grief—is what makes the moment feel real. War doesn't offer pure wins. Every step forward comes with a shadow.

The aftermath of the turning point is just as important as the moment itself. How do your characters react? Are they energized, relieved, suspicious, afraid? Do they rise to meet the new challenge, or falter under the weight of what it took to get here? Use this moment to evolve your characters. Someone who's been cautious might finally take the lead. Someone who's been driven by vengeance might find a reason to hope. Someone who was certain of their cause might start to question it. These emotional responses shape the next phase of your war drama.

A well-crafted turning point does more than just shift the direction of the story. It redefines what the story *is*. Before, it was a tale of retreat. Now it's a story of resistance. Before, it was about confidence. Now it's about survival. These transitions are where war dramas dig deepest, because they ask the characters—and the audience—to look again, rethink, and decide who they are when the world refuses to stay still.

Because in war, the turning point isn't just when the map changes. It's when the *people* change. When fear turns into courage. When doubt gives way to action. When the impossible becomes a reality—or when victory reveals the true cost of fighting at all. And if you write it right, your readers or viewers will feel the shift deep in their bones. They'll know the story will never be the same—and neither will the people living it.

Exploring Death and Loss through Character Arcs

In a war drama, death is never just a fact—it's a force. It reshapes the story, alters the emotional terrain, and leaves imprints on every character it touches. But it's not the death itself that defines the impact—it's how it affects those who live on. The story of war is the story of grief, of carrying the weight of loss, and of being changed by it. When written with care and emotional depth, death becomes more than a moment—it becomes a turning point, a mirror, and a permanent scar woven into a character's arc.

Not every war story has to be a tragedy, but every war story must acknowledge that loss is inevitable. The question isn't if a character will die—it's how, why, and what that death means to the people around them. A well-written death doesn't just close a chapter. It opens a hundred others. It reveals character. It tests resolve. It shifts tone. Sometimes it even propels the story into its next act, forcing your characters to confront something they've been avoiding all along.

There are many ways to use death in a war narrative, but the most powerful ones come when the loss lands close to home. The fallen character might be a mentor, a lover, a best friend, a younger sibling, or even someone the protagonist just met—but connected with deeply. The emotional bond between the characters is what determines the weight of the loss. The stronger the connection, the deeper the echo. And that echo is what propels your character arc.

Loss can fuel revenge, but it can also drive transformation. A once-naïve character might harden after watching someone die in their arms. A hardened soldier might break after losing someone they quietly cared for. A leader might question their decisions after watching a young recruit fall because of an order they gave. The aftermath of death is fertile ground for character growth—if you let it breathe. Don't rush it. Let the grief sit. Let it hurt. Let it take up space.

One of the most powerful tools at your disposal is *what* you choose to show. Sometimes the death is seen in detail—a slow moment full of pain, final words, held hands, or a look that says everything. Other times, the death is revealed second-hand—a letter, a discovery, a quiet admission. Both can work. It depends on the tone of your story and the perspective you want to take. But however it's revealed, the loss should *mean* something to the character's emotional arc. It should shift the way they see the world, or themselves.

You can use ChatGPT to develop arcs where loss shapes behavior over time. Try asking for, "A character arc for a soldier who loses their best friend in battle and becomes emotionally closed off," or "A resistance fighter whose lover is killed, leading to a crisis of purpose." These arcs can span your entire story or just a few key chapters, but they help you explore the *emotional physics* of death—how it ripples through relationships, memory, and motivation.

Grief shows up differently for everyone. Some characters shut down. Some explode. Some distract themselves with tasks or violence or jokes. Some try to take on the traits or mission of the person they lost, almost like trying to keep them alive. These reactions are rich with story potential. Maybe a character begins wearing the watch of a fallen comrade and can't stop checking the time. Maybe they finish the letter someone else started. Maybe they keep imagining conversations that will never happen. These actions, even if small, are loaded with emotional truth.

Death can also be symbolic. Maybe a character dies just as someone else is born. Maybe someone dies with a smile, giving peace to others in the group. Maybe a death creates a new rift or a new bond. A funeral scene in a war story is never just about mourning—it's about the living trying to make sense of what's left. What rituals do your characters hold onto? What do they say? What do they *not* say? Sometimes the silence around a death speaks louder than any speech.

You can explore character arcs that revolve entirely around death from the beginning. A character might enter the war already grieving. Another might be driven by the fear of losing someone close. The anticipation of death, and the way characters brace for it, is another form of loss. It shapes relationships, makes characters act with urgency, and creates a kind of fragile, desperate beauty in every interaction. War stories thrive on that tension—of people trying to live in a place where death is always nearby.

There's also the moment when a character is *almost* lost. These near-death moments, where someone is presumed dead or barely survives, can have just as much emotional weight as actual deaths. They allow your story to explore how grief prepares people for loss, how people change even when the loss is reversed, and how difficult it is to return from the edge of the unknown. Sometimes the person who comes back isn't the same. Sometimes the one who waited doesn't know how to let them back in.

And then, of course, there's survivor's guilt. This is one of the most haunting elements of any war drama. Why did they die instead of me? What could I have done differently? Characters carry this guilt like a phantom. It haunts their decisions. It makes them hesitate. Or it drives them harder. Let them wrestle with this—not to find closure, but to show that grief doesn't follow clean timelines. Sometimes the characters who *live* carry more pain than the ones who died.

Writing death and loss in a war drama isn't about being dramatic for the sake of it. It's about honoring the emotional truth that war changes people through grief. These losses become part of your characters' identity. They don't move on—they move forward with the weight of memory. And that weight should shape every decision, every relationship, every quiet moment that follows.

Because in the end, war stories are not just about who wins. They're about who's left. And how those who remain find ways to keep going—with ghosts beside them, with memories in their hands, and with the shadows of every lost soul etched into the choices they'll make next. That's where your story finds its emotional depth. That's where it becomes not just a war drama—but a human one.

When Heroes Fail and Cowards Rise

War has a way of breaking the rules we expect from people. It pulls apart every assumption we have about bravery and exposes the truth: that heroes fall short and cowards can surprise us. Writing these reversals—where the brave crumble and the timid rise to the moment—isn't just good drama. It's honest. It's raw. And it's where your war story becomes something much more human than just a tale of good versus evil. It becomes a story of complexity, contradiction, and unexpected strength.

The image of the fearless, self-sacrificing hero is deeply ingrained in war storytelling. But real war doesn't care about image. It doesn't care how tough someone looks or how many speeches they've given. In real combat, pressure exposes character. And that pressure doesn't always bring out the best. Sometimes the strongest, loudest, most reliable figure—the one everyone looks to—just *breaks*. They freeze. They make the wrong call. They run. And that failure is not only believable—it's necessary.

A hero's failure doesn't have to be dramatic to be devastating. It can be a small choice at the wrong time. Hesitating when action is needed. Letting fear override instinct. Refusing to take responsibility for others. Lying to protect themselves. And afterward, what really matters is how they respond. Do they shut down? Try to redeem themselves? Collapse under the guilt? Use the failure as fuel for growth? This is where the character arc deepens. The failure isn't just about that one moment—it's about how it reshapes everything after.

Meanwhile, the so-called coward—the quiet one, the fearful one, the doubter—can do something no one expected. They step up when everyone else has fallen. They make the call, take the risk, hold the line. And it doesn't come from confidence—it comes from desperation, love, instinct, or just the refusal to see anyone else die. That's what makes it powerful. Because when someone everyone underestimated finds courage in the worst possible moment, it feels earned. It feels real.

These reversals don't just challenge your characters—they challenge your audience. They force readers or viewers to question their assumptions. To reconsider what bravery really looks like. Maybe it's not the guy with the medals. Maybe it's the medic who keeps working under fire. Maybe it's the cook who carries a wounded comrade for miles. Maybe it's the deserter who comes back. These unexpected turns make war stories compelling because they reflect how unpredictable and deeply personal the experience of war really is.

You can use ChatGPT to explore these arcs by asking for scenes like, "A seasoned commander hesitates during a key battle and loses the trust of their squad," or "A frightened young soldier overcomes their fear to save someone in the field." You can create storylines where fear becomes strength, or where confidence crumbles under the weight of responsibility. Let the AI help you map out the beats: the moment of collapse, the fallout, and the slow climb back—or the acceptance that there may be no redemption.

Writing the failure of a hero doesn't mean making them weak. It means making them real. Maybe they've been carrying too much weight for too long. Maybe the pressure finally cracked them. Maybe they made a call they believed in—and it cost lives. Let them feel the consequences. Let their identity shift. And if they come back from that failure, let it be messy. Don't make it easy. Growth isn't a switch—it's a struggle.

Likewise, the rise of a coward should feel natural, not forced. Don't suddenly turn a terrified soldier into an action hero. Show the hesitation. The shaking hands. The doubt. And then show the moment where something breaks inside—or something clicks. Maybe they act not out of courage, but necessity. Maybe they act because no one else will. Maybe they don't even realize they've done something heroic until it's over. That realism makes their moment of strength land with more power than any dramatic monologue ever could.

These arcs work especially well in ensemble stories. Let your characters play off each other. One hero fails while another rises. The group dynamic shifts. Trust is tested. Leadership changes hands. These moments of upheaval reveal who the characters really are—and set the stage for new conflicts, alliances, and emotional turns. Maybe the group never forgives the failure. Maybe the rising coward never wants to be seen as a leader. That emotional friction keeps your story alive long after the battle ends.

You can also use these arcs to explore themes. If your story is about identity, then a hero's failure becomes a crisis of self. If it's about redemption, then a coward's rise becomes the heart of the narrative. These reversals give you a way to say something larger about the nature of war—that it doesn't just destroy cities. It shatters expectations, rebuilds people in unexpected shapes, and reveals truths no one wants to face.

Symbolism plays a role too. Maybe the hero drops the flag they once carried. Maybe the coward picks up a fallen friend's gear. Maybe the character who always ran away finally stands their ground. These visuals can make the emotional arc hit harder, especially if the moment reflects something seeded earlier in the story. A quiet callback. A broken promise finally kept. A scar that means something now.

In the end, the reason these arcs matter is because they remind us that war is not about labels. It's about what people do when everything is falling apart. Sometimes, the strongest fall. And sometimes, the ones you least expect carry everyone forward. That's the emotional truth that lingers. That's the story that lasts. And if you write those turns with honesty, complexity, and emotional weight, your audience won't just follow your characters—they'll *believe* them. And maybe, they'll see themselves in them too.

Writing the End of the War and What It Means

The end of a war story isn't just about victory or defeat—it's about what's *left*. It's the reckoning. The silence after the last shot. The long, aching question of what all the blood, fear, sacrifice, and survival meant. Whether the war in your story ends with a bang, a treaty, a retreat, or even a whimper, it should never feel like a closing door. It should feel like the start of a different kind of struggle—the one where characters have to live with everything that's happened.

Writing the end of the war is not about wrapping things up neatly. It's about honoring the emotional truth of the journey. In most war dramas, there's a deep cost, even in so-called victory. Cities are destroyed. Relationships are fractured. People have changed in ways they can't undo. So when you bring the war to its conclusion, you're not just ending battles—you're revealing what those battles did to the people who lived through them.

One of the most powerful ways to approach the ending is through perspective. Show the moment of peace—or surrender or collapse—through the eyes of someone who's been there from the start. A soldier stepping out of the trench and hearing birdsong again. A nurse sitting in an empty hospital room. A civilian walking through a shattered street that was once their home. Let the audience feel that transition from chaos to quiet. Not triumphant quiet—*haunted* quiet.

Victory can feel hollow. A commander might look over the battlefield and see only graves. A resistance fighter might realize they don't know how to live in peacetime. A survivor might wonder what they're supposed to do now, having lost everything that gave them purpose. This is the emotional terrain you want to explore at the end of your war drama—not just the resolution of the plot, but the *emotional cost* of that resolution.

You can also use the end to revisit your story's themes. If you wrote about loyalty, show how it held up—or didn't—when the fighting stopped. If your story was about identity, show who your protagonist has become now that the war no longer defines them. If it was about loss, show what remains. Not all endings need to be sad, but they should be *honest*. Bittersweet is often more powerful than a full triumph or complete tragedy.

There's also power in showing the *aftermath* rather than the final battle itself. Sometimes the most affecting ending is set weeks or months after the fighting ends. A reunion that doesn't go the way someone hoped. A trial. A graveyard visit. A country struggling to rebuild. A character trying to fit back into a world that doesn't quite remember what they went through. These quiet, grounded scenes carry enormous weight. They give the audience time to sit with the consequences.

Use symbolism in your closing moments. The return of green grass where there was once mud. The ringing of a church bell. The rebuilding of a broken bridge. A soldier removing their uniform. A child picking up a toy left behind during an evacuation. These images speak volumes. They suggest recovery, remembrance, or even just the passage of time—without needing heavy exposition. When used subtly, they can make the end of the war feel real without saying a word.

You can also leave certain things unresolved. That's how real wars often end—not with every question answered, but with new ones asked. Who is held accountable? Who gets to write the history? What do the survivors do next? Sometimes the most powerful ending is one that feels uneasy. A smile that doesn't reach the eyes. A return home that doesn't feel like home anymore. Let your characters carry some of the war with them—because that's what people do.

ChatGPT can help you brainstorm emotionally resonant endings by prompting it with phrases like, "Write the final scene of a war story from the perspective of a soldier returning to a ruined village," or "Describe a quiet moment between two survivors after a ceasefire is declared." These scenes don't need to be epic. In fact, the smaller they are, the more they tend to hurt—and heal.

Closure in a war drama isn't about restoring what was lost. It's about showing what's changed and what the characters must carry forward. Maybe they're trying to rebuild. Maybe they're choosing forgiveness. Maybe they're walking away from everything. Maybe they're just sitting in silence, remembering the faces of those who didn't make it. All of these are endings. All of them are valid. All of them speak to the truth that war ends *differently* for everyone.

You might also explore how the world reacts. How do governments respond to the peace? How do communities treat returning veterans? How is memory preserved—or erased? Is there justice, or just more silence? These questions don't have to be answered directly, but even hinting at them gives your story a larger frame. It shows that the end of one war is rarely the end of conflict altogether. It often leads to new battles—internal, political, personal.

Ultimately, the end of the war in your story should reflect everything the characters have gone through. It should carry the emotional echoes of every choice, every loss, every moment of courage or fear. It should feel like something has ended—but not like everything has. Because life goes on after war, even if it's not the life anyone expected. And when you show that truth with depth, restraint, and emotional honesty, your audience won't just understand the story—they'll *feel* it. They'll carry it with them. Just like your characters do.

Aftermath: What Happens When the Guns Go Silent

The final shot has been fired. The treaty has been signed. The uniforms are stained, the weapons discarded or locked away, and the roar of gunfire has faded into silence. But if you're writing a war drama that lingers long after the last battle, then you know this simple truth: war doesn't end when the guns go silent. It changes shape. It moves from battlefield to memory, from violence to recovery, and from the external wreckage of cities and bodies to the internal wreckage of people trying to remember who they were before it all began.

The aftermath is often where the most powerful emotional material lives. This is the territory where you explore the long-term impact of the war on individuals, families, and entire societies. The focus shifts from survival to reckoning. From doing what it takes to stay alive, to figuring out how to live with what's been done. This is where the consequences become clear, where the trauma begins to speak, and where your characters must confront not just what happened—but who they've become in the process.

For a soldier, the end of the war doesn't mean peace. It means readjustment. Civilians may expect gratitude, but what they don't see is the insomnia, the nightmares, the guilt, the sense of dislocation. A character who used to be a leader on the battlefield may feel useless in peacetime. Someone who lived on adrenaline may feel like they've been dropped into a world that moves too slowly, too quietly. And some may try to return to normal life only to discover there is no "normal" left for them. The aftermath is not a homecoming—it's often a ghost story, told from the perspective of those who came back changed.

For civilians, the aftermath is just as complex. Buildings can be rebuilt, but communities take longer. There are gaps where people used to be. There's grief where there once was routine. Civilians who resisted may now be viewed as heroes—or punished by the new regime. Those who collaborated may try to hide or justify their actions. Children who grew up during the war may not know anything else. These threads offer rich material to explore, especially if your story focuses on relationships, generational trauma, or the slow rebuilding of trust.

And then there are the questions no one knows how to answer. Who gets to write the history of the war? Who gets to lead in the peace that follows? What happens to those caught in the middle? Are war crimes prosecuted, or brushed under the rug? Are reparations made? Are memorials built? The silence after the guns is never truly quiet—it's full of unresolved tension, of people trying to make sense of the senseless.

You can use ChatGPT to explore this phase of your story from different character angles. Ask for scenes like, "A soldier returning to his childhood home to find everything has changed," or "A war widow visiting a memorial years later." Try building from the emotional core: What does your character want now that the war is over—and what stands in the way? That's the new conflict. Not survival, but *continuation*. Not escape, but endurance.

Symbolism can be a powerful way to show the weight of the aftermath. A field of unburied helmets. A building half-reconstructed with scorched walls still visible. A scar on a character's body that still aches when the weather shifts. These physical reminders of the war's presence can be more impactful than dialogue. Let the landscape carry memory. Let the characters see it and react—sometimes silently, sometimes explosively.

The aftermath is also a time when truth begins to surface. Characters may finally admit what they did—or didn't do. Secrets come out. Betrayals are revealed. Heroes are unmasked. The emotional terrain shifts as people try to reconcile their war selves with their post-war reality. Some may seek redemption. Others might try to forget. Some may build something new from the ashes. Others may walk away, broken. All of these paths are valid, and they each add layers to your narrative.

Don't rush this part of the story. The temptation after the war ends is to wrap things up, to bring closure. But real closure doesn't come quickly. Let grief have space. Let confusion sit on the surface. Let healing be slow and uncertain. That's what gives your war drama its emotional weight. The guns may be silent, but the echoes remain.

You can also explore how the aftermath affects relationships. Couples that were held together by the war may find they no longer recognize each other. Friendships forged in combat may not survive peace. Families torn apart may try to reconnect, only to realize the distance has become too wide. These emotional stories are deeply human, and they ground your narrative in something real—something the audience can feel in their chest, even if they've never experienced war themselves.

Sometimes, the most powerful scene in your story is the one where a character sits quietly and doesn't know what to do next. Because that's the truth for so many people when the war ends. The purpose that kept them going is gone. The rules have changed. And the silence feels heavier than the noise ever did.

So, when you write the aftermath, don't treat it as an epilogue. Treat it as the heart of the story's truth. This is where the characters face themselves fully for the first time. This is where the ghosts gather. This is where memory, regret, and fragile hope collide. And when you write those moments with honesty and restraint, you give your war story a closing chapter that doesn't just end the narrative—it *honors* it.

Because war might stop with silence, but it's what people do *after* the silence that reveals who they really are.

Writing a Bittersweet Resolution

In a war drama, a perfectly happy ending can feel dishonest—and a completely tragic one can feel overwhelming. But somewhere between triumph and despair lies the most powerful emotional landing zone: the bittersweet resolution. This kind of ending resonates deeply because it mirrors real life. In war, even the victories come with scars. There are moments of light, but they're surrounded by shadow. When you write a bittersweet resolution, you're giving your audience something to feel that lives beyond the final page or scene—something that lingers, like an echo.

A bittersweet ending doesn't mean everything is left unresolved. It means there's a balance between what's gained and what's lost. The war might be over, but the cost is still present. A character may survive but carry permanent damage—physical, emotional, or both. A goal may be achieved, but a relationship might not survive. Peace may come, but justice may not. These contradictions are the emotional DNA of a good war story ending, and they make the resolution feel earned rather than imposed.

The key to crafting this kind of ending is emotional honesty. Don't force hope where it doesn't belong—but don't bury it, either. Let the characters who deserve peace find a version of it, even if it's incomplete. Let those who paid the highest prices feel the ache of what could have been. You want to show that life continues, but not in the way anyone imagined. That's the heartbreak—and the beauty—of it.

To find your bittersweet tone, ask yourself what each character wanted at the beginning of the story—and what they actually have now. Often, what they get is not what they wanted, but what they needed. Or they get what they wanted, but it no longer feels like victory. A soldier comes home to find their town intact, but their family gone. A resistance leader wins the war, but loses their faith. A young recruit becomes a hero, but feels numb. These are not failures—they are emotional conclusions that speak to growth, consequence, and complexity.

You can use ChatGPT to test different variations of bittersweet endings. Prompt it with ideas like, "Write the final scene where a soldier returns home to an empty house but finds a letter waiting," or "Describe the final moment of a resistance fighter who sees peace but can't feel it." Use the AI to explore the range of what *could* happen, and then pick the ending that feels most emotionally truthful to your characters.

Symbolism is your ally here. Maybe a character visits a grave and plants a flower. Maybe a war medal is tucked away in a drawer. Maybe a soldier gives their boots to a passing child. These small gestures carry enormous weight. They suggest change, reflection, and emotional movement without the need for dramatic speeches. The quieter the moment, the deeper it often lands.

Dialogue in a bittersweet resolution should be minimal and careful. Let characters speak from exhaustion, not clarity. Let them feel more than they can say. A final "I'm sorry" can say more than a whole monologue. A line like "I thought it would feel different" after a long-awaited victory hits harder than any toast or celebration. You want the audience to feel the emotion underneath the words—the hesitation, the sadness, the gratitude, the grief.

This type of ending is also a place to bring your themes full circle. If your story has been about the cost of loyalty, then end with a moment that shows how much it hurt—but also how much it mattered. If your story is about identity, let your protagonist show who they've become without needing to say it. Bittersweet resolutions don't explain—they *reveal.*

Characters might part ways instead of reuniting. They might find closure in the form of letting go. They might finally cry, finally sleep, finally say nothing at all. Don't be afraid of restraint. Let silence and stillness carry meaning. These are endings that trust your audience. They don't need everything tied up. They need to *feel* something true.

One way to structure a bittersweet resolution is to give your characters a small win—but remind the audience of what it cost. A soldier finds their missing sister, but she's no longer the same. A city is liberated, but the ones who made it possible aren't there to see it. A wedding takes place, but one seat at the table is left empty. These contrasts give the audience the release they crave—without denying the emotional truth of the story.

Even visually, if you're writing for screen, a bittersweet tone can be conveyed through lighting, color, and pacing. A warm sunrise over a ruined landscape. Children playing in the background as adults stand in silence. Laughter and tears in the same frame. These contrasts are what give the ending its power. Because they acknowledge that peace isn't pure, and neither is grief.

Ultimately, a bittersweet resolution is about dignity. It says the characters didn't get everything they wanted, but they got something. That they paid dearly, but they made it through. That the world is still broken, but there's hope in the cracks. It's an ending that hurts in all the right ways—and comforts without pretending to heal everything.

In war, there are no clean slates. But there *can* be new beginnings. Your job as a writer is to show what they look like, through the tears, the silence, the small smiles, and the quiet goodbyes. If you've done your work throughout the story, then by the time you reach this final chapter, your characters will carry the full weight of the war—and so will your audience. That's what makes a bittersweet ending unforgettable. Not because it's happy. Not because it's sad. But because it's *real*.

Using ChatGPT to Fill Historical Gaps

When you're writing a war drama—especially one set in a specific historical period—you're going to come up against gaps. Maybe it's a missing detail about a specific battle. Maybe it's the daily life of a soldier, a resistance fighter, a civilian under occupation. Maybe it's the exact look of a uniform, the rations people survived on, or the emotional tone of a letter home. You'll find yourself searching for details that are hard to locate or locked behind paywalls, archives, or hours of deep reading. That's where ChatGPT becomes one of your most valuable allies—not just as a writing assistant, but as a creative and historical bridge.

Using ChatGPT to fill historical gaps doesn't mean abandoning accuracy. It means giving yourself a tool to quickly generate reasonable, well-informed context you can build on, refine, or fact-check later. It's about momentum—keeping your story moving while still respecting the truth of the time period. The secret is in how you ask and how you use what you're given.

Let's say you're writing a war drama set in North Africa during World War II, and your character is a British tank commander. You want to describe what it felt like inside a tank during a sandstorm, but you can't find first-hand accounts right away. You can prompt ChatGPT with something like, "Describe what it was like to operate a British tank in a sandstorm during the North Africa campaign in 1942." You'll get a quick atmospheric draft with sensory details, conditions, likely equipment, and challenges that you can either use as-is or rework in your own voice.

You can also ask for daily life details: "What food did French civilians eat during the Nazi occupation?" or "Describe the gear a Soviet soldier would carry during winter in Stalingrad." You'll be given a compact overview that saves hours of scattered searching and gives you a foundation to build your scene. These aren't replacements for deep research when needed—but they're your creative jumpstart, helping you push past inertia and stay in flow.

Sometimes it's not just about facts—it's about tone, perspective, and human behavior. Ask ChatGPT, "What emotions might a teenage soldier in Vietnam have felt on their first patrol?" and you'll get not just descriptions but insight into psychological context, social pressure, and personal fears. These are the emotional colors that help paint your war drama with realism and resonance.

Another way to use ChatGPT is for creating composites or representative characters based on the types of people who would've lived through a particular moment in history. Try, "Create a character who is a nurse in a field hospital during the Korean War," or "Invent a resistance courier working in Amsterdam in 1943." You'll get personality traits, background, context, and details you might not have thought to research. Even if you don't use the AI's version directly, it will spark new ideas and help you think more deeply about who your characters are and what shaped them.

You can also ask ChatGPT to simulate documents, dialogue, or correspondence in a given historical voice. Say you need a letter from a soldier in World War I to his sister. Prompt with, "Write a letter from a British soldier on the front lines of the Somme in 1916 to his younger sister, trying to reassure her while not revealing the horror." You'll receive a period-appropriate, emotionally nuanced draft that you can tweak into your character's voice. These kinds of personalized pieces can make your story more intimate and emotionally textured.

Don't hesitate to push for alternate perspectives either. Ask, "How might a German civilian mother have felt during the final days of World War II in Berlin?" or "What thoughts would a Japanese-American internee have had in a U.S. internment camp during the 1940s?" This allows you to write beyond the typical lens of history and bring in voices that are often underrepresented or overlooked. ChatGPT doesn't just help you fill gaps—it can help you *expand* the frame of your story.

The tool also shines when you're writing fictional wars based on real ones. If your story takes place in a fictional world with a war similar to Vietnam, ask, "Describe a war similar to the Vietnam War, with guerrilla tactics and jungle terrain, in a fictional setting." You'll get ideas that borrow from real historical conflicts without being tied to one specific event. This is great for writers who want historical realism with a layer of creative flexibility.

Of course, it's important to remember that ChatGPT is trained on a wide range of data and can occasionally get things wrong or oversimplify. So treat it as a smart collaborator, not a final authority. Use it to generate plausible drafts and outlines, but fact-check anything that plays a critical role in your plot or setting. Think of it as your creative research assistant—fast, flexible, and tireless.

Another useful trick: if you're stuck on how to describe a historical object, practice, or environment, don't just ask for the facts—ask for the *experience*. "What did it feel like to sleep in a trench in World War I?" will get you closer to something you can use dramatically than "Describe a trench." And the more specific you get, the more helpful the output will be.

Finally, remember that your story is not a history textbook. It's a human drama that lives in the details, the emotion, and the texture of real or inspired events. ChatGPT helps you bridge the gaps so you can focus on what matters most—your characters, their choices, their relationships, and the way war changes them. Whether you're recreating real events or inventing fictional ones inspired by history, this tool helps you write with confidence, momentum, and depth.

So the next time you find yourself stuck in a gap, staring at a blank page and wondering how it *actually* felt to march through snow in the Ardennes or how a Morse code message might sound in the dead of night—ask ChatGPT. It might not be perfect, but it'll get you close enough to feel something. And in storytelling, that's what counts.

Working with ChatGPT to Write Realistic Battle Scenes

Writing a compelling battle scene is one of the greatest challenges in any war drama. It's not just about gunfire, explosions, or tactical maneuvers—it's about *immersion*. The reader or viewer doesn't want a sterile account of troop movements. They want to *feel* the chaos, the confusion, the fear, the adrenaline, the grit in a soldier's teeth, the panic in their gut. A battle scene done right is overwhelming in all the best ways—and ChatGPT can be a powerful partner in getting you there.

The first step to writing a realistic battle scene with ChatGPT is to define your needs clearly. What kind of battle are you writing? Is it a historical engagement based on real events, like D-Day or the Battle of Stalingrad? Or is it a fictional battle inspired by real warfare, like a mountain ambush in a made-up civil war or a night-time raid by insurgents? Give ChatGPT the who, where, and when. You can prompt it with something like: "Write a gritty, realistic description of a battle between U.S. Marines and entrenched enemy forces in a jungle setting during a fictional Southeast Asian conflict."

From that prompt, you'll get an intense, sensory-laden draft. You'll see the terrain, hear the bullets whizzing by, feel the rain-soaked boots, and taste the metallic dryness in the back of a soldier's throat. These are the raw materials you can reshape, trim, and inject with your character's voice or viewpoint. What you're aiming for is realism that isn't just technical—but emotional and physical.

One effective way to work with ChatGPT is to break the scene into pieces. You can prompt for individual moments or actions. For instance, ask:

"Describe the opening seconds of an ambush in a dense forest at dawn."

Or: "Write a scene where a squad is pinned down and calling for artillery support."

Or even: "Give me a moment of silence right before a major charge begins."

These specific prompts help you build the scene beat by beat. They allow you to control pacing and tension, layering intensity rather than dumping a chaotic mess of action all at once. You don't want your battle to read like a list of explosions—you want it to rise, collapse, twist, and turn like a living, terrifying moment.

You can also use ChatGPT to write from different character perspectives. Maybe one character is a commander viewing the battle from a hilltop, trying to make impossible decisions. Another is a medic crawling through blood-soaked mud to reach the wounded. A third is a terrified new recruit doing everything wrong, just trying to survive. By shifting perspectives, you reveal the human experience of battle—the mistakes, the courage, the terror, and the heartbreak.

Ask ChatGPT for tone adjustments, too. You can prompt it to revise a scene for more emotional impact, more physical detail, more panic, more noise, more silence. A good follow-up might be, "Rewrite the same battle scene from the perspective of a soldier suffering from tunnel vision due to fear." You'll get a tighter, more psychologically intense version that you can blend into your character's arc.

Don't forget the emotional aftermath. Ask for scenes immediately following the clash, like:

"Describe a soldier stumbling away from a battlefield, dazed and wounded, as the smoke clears."

Or: "Write a moment of reflection between two surviving soldiers as they look over the carnage."

These quieter, more intimate moments contrast beautifully with the chaos and give the reader space to process what just happened.

You can also explore how to write the sounds, smells, and physical sensations of battle. Try prompts like:

"What does a battlefield smell like after heavy artillery?"

Or: "Describe the feeling of trying to reload a rifle while under suppressive fire."

These add the sensory realism that separates an average action scene from an unforgettable war moment.

And for historical or tactical accuracy, ChatGPT can serve up useful overviews in a flash. Ask for common tactics used during urban warfare in WWII, or the challenges of fighting in trench conditions. If your story includes real battles, you can have ChatGPT outline those engagements to give you a frame for your fictional version. The more you understand the actual flow of these events, the more confident you'll feel bending them to your dramatic needs.

Another underrated use of ChatGPT is helping with choreography. If you're not familiar with how squads move, how ambushes are structured, or how close-quarter combat works, ask directly:

"How would a team of five soldiers breach a building held by enemy forces?"

Or: "What are the standard hand signals used in small unit tactics?"

You don't have to become a military expert overnight—you just need enough of the vocabulary and logic to make your battle scenes believable.

Finally, remember the heart of a great battle scene is not the shooting. It's the people. The relationships. The fear. The decisions made under impossible pressure. Ask ChatGPT to simulate moral conflict inside the fight.

Try: "Write a scene where a soldier hesitates to shoot a young enemy combatant and pays the price,"

Or: "A character has to choose between staying to save a wounded friend or retreating with their squad."

This is where the emotional stakes rise to match the physical ones—and where your story really punches through.

ChatGPT isn't here to write your war story for you. It's here to hand you bricks, mortar, and blueprints. You choose the shape. You choose the emotion. You decide where the camera points. But when you're knee-deep in writing, exhausted, stuck, or just needing a new angle on how to bring battle to life, this tool can save hours of struggle and reignite your momentum.

So don't be afraid to get gritty, emotional, and specific in your requests. The more clearly you shape your intent, the more powerfully ChatGPT can help you recreate what war feels like—not just what it looks like. And in war drama, that difference is everything.

Balancing Fact and Fiction

Writing a war drama means constantly walking a tightrope between truth and storytelling. On one side is the hard reality—dates, battles, uniforms, the brutal facts of history. On the other is the freedom to invent characters, imagine emotional journeys, and build arcs that serve your narrative. Stray too far into fantasy, and your story risks losing credibility. Stick too closely to fact, and you might end up with a history lesson instead of a compelling drama. The real art lies in the balance—blending fact and fiction so seamlessly that your story feels authentic, emotionally true, and dramatically satisfying.

The first step to finding that balance is knowing *what kind of war story* you're writing. Are you telling a fictional tale set during a real conflict like World War II or the Vietnam War? Are you building a completely invented conflict inspired by historical events? Or are you blending real people and events with fictional ones to explore emotional truth in a heightened way? Each approach gives you different boundaries—and freedoms—to work within.

If you're writing within a known historical period, accuracy matters. You want to respect the lived experiences of those who were there. That means getting the basics right: the geography, the timeline, the technology, the structure of military units, and the major events. If you place a fictional character in the Normandy invasion, that's fine—but make sure the beach they land on existed, that the timeline checks out, and that the tone of the battle reflects historical truth. These details ground your story and earn the trust of your audience.

But don't get stuck thinking historical accuracy means just quoting facts. Emotional accuracy is just as important. Your characters should *feel* like they belong in the world you're building. That means understanding how people spoke, thought, and behaved in that era. What did they fear? What did they hope for? How did they handle trauma or grief? Use historical research to inform these layers of character, even when the characters themselves are fictional.

You can use ChatGPT to check historical consistency while keeping your creativity intact. Ask things like, "What kind of weapons would a German infantry soldier use in 1943?" or "What were the conditions like in a Pacific island campaign?" You'll get details that can shape your scene, even if your characters are fictional. And if you're working in a fictional war, you can still borrow realism from real-world analogs. For instance, if your invented civil war mirrors the Spanish Civil War, study that conflict to inspire the atmosphere, alliances, betrayals, and tragedies.

When you create fictional characters in a real conflict, be clear about how they fit into history. Did they witness a major event? Did they influence it? Did they move through it unnoticed? The more you weave your fictional story around the real events—without trying to rewrite those events—the more believable it will be. A fictional nurse in a real field hospital. A spy on the edge of a known assassination plot. A soldier who missed the main battle by hours but still suffers the aftermath. These stories feel rooted and personal, without needing to contradict the known record.

The best war dramas often mix real and invented with care. A fictional squad might be part of a real division. A real operation might be seen through the eyes of characters who never existed. Or the reverse—a real person might interact with invented people, offering a more intimate take on what history books often miss. If you use a real historical figure, treat them with respect. Base their words and actions on known behavior and philosophy, but don't be afraid to explore their humanity. Everyone in history had doubts, fears, and contradictions.

Fictionalizing war gives you space to explore *what could have happened.* It lets you tell the untold stories—the ones history forgot or couldn't confirm. A child caught in the crossfire. A woman smuggling messages. A deserter trying to find peace. These characters might not be in textbooks, but they represent emotional truths that many lived. That's the gift of fiction: it can fill in the emotional gaps and amplify the human voice within the vast, impersonal machinery of war.

When blending fact and fiction, transparency matters too. If you're writing a novel or screenplay that fictionalizes a real conflict, consider including a note about what's real and what's invented. Not as an apology—but as a gesture of respect. Many readers or viewers appreciate knowing how you approached the balance, and it reinforces your commitment to truth, even through imagination.

Be careful not to use fiction to gloss over harsh truths. War is ugly, cruel, and complex. Don't invent a heroic ending that contradicts the real tragedy. Don't whitewash historical crimes or rewrite events in a way that makes villains into saints. You can invent characters who find hope—but let that hope live alongside grief. Let your fiction add layers, not erase them.

One of the best ways to keep balance is to constantly ask: *Does this feel emotionally true?* Whether it actually happened doesn't always matter. What matters is that it could have. That your readers believe in it. That your characters act in ways that make sense for the world and the time. That their choices, victories, and failures feel real. That's what keeps your fiction grounded, even when it flies.

Using ChatGPT can help you cross-check facts, brainstorm plausible fictional events, and write scenes that are anchored in history. You can try prompts like, "Create a fictional soldier's experience during the Battle of the Bulge," or "Describe a love story that unfolds during the London Blitz." These scenes don't rewrite history—they breathe life into it.

In the end, the line between fact and fiction isn't a wall—it's a conversation. A dance. A collaboration between what *was* and what *might have been*. When you find that balance, your war drama doesn't just entertain—it *matters*. It teaches. It reveals. It remembers. And in that space between the real and the imagined, you can create something that feels more human—and more lasting—than either alone ever could.

How to Use AI to Generate Emotional Beats

War drama lives and dies by its emotional beats. These are the moments when the audience leans forward, holds their breath, or feels their chest tighten. They're not just about what's happening—they're about what it *feels* like. A good emotional beat can be the space between dialogue, the crack in a soldier's voice, the silence before a command, or the whispered memory of someone who didn't make it. These beats give your war story weight and texture. They humanize the plot. And one of the most effective ways to generate them quickly, deeply, and creatively is by working with AI.

ChatGPT, when used well, can help you explore emotional territory without falling back on clichés. It won't just tell you that someone is "sad" or "afraid"—if prompted right, it can offer layered, character-specific moments of emotional resonance. The trick is in asking not for broad feelings, but for *precise emotional moments*. Instead of asking, "Write a sad scene," try, "Describe a soldier realizing their best friend is missing after a bombing raid." The more context you give, the more nuanced the emotional response you'll get.

To use AI to generate emotional beats, start by building around the *emotional arc* of your character. What are they feeling in this chapter? What just happened to them, and what's coming next? Let's say your protagonist just survived an ambush, but lost someone in their unit. You can prompt ChatGPT with, "Write a short internal monologue of a soldier who just made it out of an ambush alive but can't stop thinking about the person who didn't make it." From that, you'll get something raw and grounded—something you can mold to fit the tone and rhythm of your story.

Another great way to develop emotional beats with ChatGPT is by focusing on *non-verbal emotion*. Instead of just writing, "He was afraid," try prompting, "Describe what fear feels like in the body of a soldier hiding in a trench, listening to enemy footsteps get closer." You'll get descriptions of heartbeat, breath, sweat, and the struggle to stay still. These details let your readers feel the emotion instead of just reading about it.

You can also ask the AI to offer multiple versions of an emotional beat so you can choose the one that best suits your character. Try, "Give me three different emotional reactions a war nurse might have after losing a patient in surgery," or "Write a short scene showing how a resistance fighter tries to hide their grief in front of their team." This lets you explore different tonal approaches—stoic, explosive, numbed, bitter—and find what feels most authentic.

Let's talk about using AI to explore *emotional contrast*, which is where the real dramatic punch often lies. A soldier might joke moments before a grenade hits. A couple might share a kiss in the middle of a bombing raid. A parent might quietly fix a child's hair while preparing to evacuate a city. These juxtapositions make emotions hit harder. Prompt ChatGPT with, "Give me a tender moment between two characters while artillery shells fall in the distance," or "Write a scene where a soldier tries to celebrate their birthday while on patrol." These emotionally layered beats are where your characters come alive.

AI can also help you with *repressed emotion*—which is especially common in war stories, where characters often hide what they feel to survive. Ask for, "A dialogue between two soldiers who avoid talking about what just happened but clearly feel the weight of it," and you'll get a scene built on subtext. These are some of the most compelling emotional beats because they demand more from the audience. You're showing, not telling. You're letting silence speak.

It's also worth using AI to generate emotional *aftermath*. The battle is over. The loss is real. The silence settles. What now? Ask, "Write a scene where a character stands over the ruins of their hometown and doesn't know what to feel," or "Describe a group of survivors eating quietly after a night of fighting." These are low-energy but high-impact moments. They create space for the audience to reflect with the characters.

Another technique: generate beats in *parallel perspectives*. Ask ChatGPT to write the same emotional moment from two points of view. For instance, "A father saying goodbye to his son before the son leaves for war—from the father's perspective," and then, "The same scene from the son's perspective." You'll get contrasting internal worlds that can enrich your character dynamics and give you ideas for layered interactions and dialogue.

You can even use AI to brainstorm emotional "mini-beats" that aren't full scenes—just fragments. Try asking for, "Give me ten emotionally charged actions a character might take to express silent grief." You might get things like cleaning someone's boots, folding an old uniform, touching a photo but not looking at it. These are the kinds of details that give your story life between the lines.

And if you're stuck? Ask ChatGPT to analyze an emotional arc. For example, say, "In a story where a soldier is slowly losing faith in the cause, what emotional beats could mark that change?" The AI will lay out a progression: doubt, hesitation, a quiet breakdown, a confrontation, a moment of despair. You can use this to shape your scenes with a better sense of rhythm and build-up.

In the end, emotional beats are about timing, texture, and truth. They don't need to be big to be powerful—they just need to be *felt*. With ChatGPT, you can experiment freely, try new angles, and explore emotional states that surprise even you. It won't replace your storytelling instincts—but it will sharpen them, support them, and keep them moving when you need that extra push.

So the next time your story feels flat or too focused on plot, take a breath and dive into the emotion. Ask ChatGPT to show you what the characters aren't saying. What they're feeling in their hands, their throat, their silence. Because that's where the story really lives—in the beats between the bullets, in the moments no one speaks, in the things they carry long after the war is done.

Letting Your Characters Drive the Plot

In a war drama, it's tempting to let the war itself take the lead. The battles, the politics, the movements of armies—they're dramatic, powerful, and full of narrative potential. But if you want your story to resonate, you can't let the plot pull your characters around like pawns on a board. It has to be the other way around. Your characters—flawed, brave, frightened, hopeful, desperate—are the engine of the story. The war is just the setting that turns up the heat.

Letting your characters drive the plot means shifting your mindset from "What happens next?" to "What would this character *do* next, and why?" Every decision, every action, every moment of silence or confrontation should come from what the character wants, what they fear, and what they're struggling with inside. When you write like that, the story unfolds naturally, and the emotional beats hit harder because they're earned—not imposed.

You might start with a rough outline—maybe you know you want to reach a major battle, a betrayal, a peace treaty, or a reunion. But how you get there should depend on your characters' choices. If your protagonist is a young soldier, terrified but determined to protect his brother, then his decisions in combat won't be about strategy—they'll be about *that relationship*. If he hears his brother's voice down the hill during an ambush, he might abandon his post to help. That's not just drama—it's character driving plot.

Use ChatGPT to help test different character-based plot decisions. Try something like, "If a soldier finds out their commanding officer is planning to sacrifice a unit for a strategic gain, what might they do if they've already lost someone they loved to a similar decision?" The AI will give you options—confront the officer, warn the unit, go through with it but regret it. These aren't just plot turns. They're emotional expressions. They make the story feel alive because they come from the inside out.

When you're not sure where the plot should go next, stop and ask: What does this character *want* right now? What are they willing to do to get it? And what's standing in their way? That tension between desire and obstacle is the real engine of your plot. And in war, that tension gets amplified. The stakes are higher. The cost is steeper. But the core principle stays the same: plot is what your characters *do* under pressure.

Think of every major plot point in your story as a reaction to a choice. A betrayal happens not because the script demands one—but because a character feels unseen, pushed too far, or tempted by something they need. A retreat happens not because the army loses—but because the protagonist finally accepts they can't save everyone. These plot moments don't just move the story—they deepen it.

You can use AI to explore what different characters might do in the same situation. Ask, "How would a guilt-ridden commander react to losing another soldier?" versus, "How would a soldier with something to prove react to the same event?" You'll start to see how emotional makeup creates narrative pathways. One choice leads to confrontation. The other leads to silence, shame, and maybe self-destruction. Those paths *are* your plot.

Characters should also drive the pacing of your story. If your protagonist is spiraling emotionally, slow the story down. Let scenes breathe. Let things fall apart. If they're desperate and decisive, tighten the rhythm—short scenes, quick cuts, urgent dialogue. Let their mindset shape how the story feels. It's not just about what happens—it's how it *feels to them*. That's what the audience will remember.

This approach also helps you avoid cliché. War dramas are full of familiar beats—last stands, heroic speeches, tragic deaths. But when those moments come from a specific character's choices, they never feel recycled. They feel personal.

A character who sacrifices themselves doesn't do it because it's "the right moment"—they do it because everything in their arc has led them there. It's not about ticking a box. It's about paying off the emotional journey.

And don't be afraid to let characters derail your plot in the best way. Sometimes they'll surprise you. A character who was supposed to be a background figure steps forward and changes everything. A character meant to survive makes a choice that gets them killed. These moments may push your outline off course—but they usually make your story stronger, richer, and more alive. Trust your characters. They know where they're going.

You can also use ChatGPT to play out dialogue-driven decisions. Ask for a scene where two characters argue about whether to retreat or keep fighting, each driven by a different emotional motivation. Then see where the scene leads. You may find the conflict reveals a truth you hadn't considered. And suddenly, the next scene becomes clear—not because of plot logic, but because of emotional truth.

Letting your characters drive the plot doesn't mean giving up control. It means shifting the focus. You're still shaping the story, but you're shaping it *from the inside out*. You're letting character choices determine direction, not external events. And in a war story, that's where the real depth lives—not in the size of the explosions, but in the decisions made in the moments between them.

So the next time you're outlining a chapter or planning the next scene, pause and ask not "What needs to happen?" but "What *would* happen if this person—after everything they've been through—had to choose?" That's where the story is. That's where the emotion is. And that's how you write a war drama that people feel in their bones. Because it's not just about war—it's about *who we are when the world falls apart*, and what we choose to do next.

Using Letters, Journals, and Found Footage as Devices

In war dramas, emotion often hides between the gunfire and explosions, waiting for a quieter moment to be heard. That's where letters, journals, and found footage become powerful storytelling devices. They offer something war rarely does: intimacy. These fragments of personal history give your audience a glimpse into your characters' minds and hearts—often revealing things that couldn't be spoken aloud. When used thoughtfully, they can transform your story from a war narrative into a deeply human experience.

Let's start with letters. There's a long literary and cinematic tradition of soldiers writing letters home, and for good reason. Letters are where your characters drop the mask. They're a safe space to express fear, love, guilt, or hope—things they wouldn't admit out loud in a trench or at a strategy table. A letter lets you reveal a character's inner world with vulnerability. A tough sergeant might write to his daughter about the stars. A resistance fighter might write to a lover they may never see again. A letter might be sent—or it might be found later, unsent and crumpled in a pocket. Either way, it carries the weight of something unfinished, something deeply personal.

Journals work differently. They're less curated, less performative. While letters are written for someone else, journals are written for no one. That's why they can be raw, messy, and painfully honest. A journal entry might contradict a character's behavior in public. A commander who shows no emotion on the battlefield might write about his mounting panic, his dreams, his regrets. A nurse might describe the unbearable routine of tending to the dying. These moments pull your audience deeper into the characters, creating a contrast between what the world sees and what the character truly feels.

ChatGPT is a great tool for crafting letters and journal entries in your characters' voices. Try prompts like, "Write a journal entry by a young soldier on the night before a doomed offensive," or "Create a letter from a medic to their mother, trying to describe the war without scaring her." You'll get emotionally rich material that you can fine-tune into something authentic. Use these entries to build character arcs, to foreshadow future events, or to reflect on choices already made.

Now let's talk about found footage. This can be a literal device—video recordings, audio logs, or photographs—or a narrative one, like a discovered diary or document that reframes everything. Found footage can be used to tell a parallel story, to reveal a hidden truth, or to let the past speak for itself. A photo found in a burned-out village might raise questions about who lived there. A helmet cam video might show a different side of a battle than the official report. These artifacts create mystery, tension, and depth.

You can even use found materials to structure your entire story. A narrative might unfold as a collection of documents—a series of letters between soldiers and their families, or a war journal passed from one character to another. This epistolary structure lets the audience piece together the bigger picture through the emotional puzzle pieces left behind. It's a great way to build a layered, immersive experience, especially when multiple voices tell the story.

One of the most powerful uses of these devices is *contradiction*. What a character says in a letter may not match what we see them do. What's written in a journal might hide as much as it reveals. Found footage might cast doubt on what others claim. These contradictions build dramatic irony and emotional complexity. They challenge the audience to decide what to believe—and who to trust.

These devices also slow the pace in the best way. War stories are often fast, chaotic, and loud. But letters and journals invite stillness. They give your characters room to breathe and reflect. A single sentence—"I'm sorry I left things the way

I did"—can hit harder than a battlefield explosion. These moments allow the audience to catch their breath too, and to process the emotional toll of the war right alongside the characters.

You can use these devices for subtle worldbuilding, too. A shopping list scrawled in the margin of a resistance fighter's notebook. A child's drawing tucked inside a soldier's kit. An old recording that keeps playing on a loop in a ruined city. These aren't exposition—they're emotion disguised as texture. They say more about the world than dialogue ever could.

Another benefit of using letters, journals, and found footage is that they open up new narrative voices. Your protagonist doesn't have to tell the whole story. Maybe a forgotten journal gives us a glimpse into the life of a character who died early on. Maybe a letter is found too late to change the outcome. These voices—sometimes silent in the present—can still echo throughout the story, influencing choices, haunting survivors, or bringing long-buried truths to light.

You can also use ChatGPT to generate layers of these devices across time. Ask it for a soldier's first letter home—and then one six months later, after loss and trauma have reshaped them. Ask for a journal entry before a mission, and another after, when things didn't go as planned. You'll see the evolution, the wear and tear on the psyche, the heartbreak of someone who's trying to hold on to something human in an inhuman time.

And when you do include these devices in your war drama, let them matter. Don't just use them as decoration. Let a letter change someone's mind. Let a found photo lead to a revelation. Let a journal entry spark conflict, confession, or catharsis. These aren't just emotional add-ons. They are fuel for character decisions, emotional beats, and turning points in your story.

Ultimately, letters, journals, and found footage bring your war drama down to earth. They remind the audience that behind every battle is a person. Behind every statistic is a story. And behind every soldier is someone writing down the truth—even if it never gets sent, or heard, or read aloud. These devices help you whisper the parts of the story that would otherwise be lost in the noise. And that whisper, in the right hands, can be louder than any gun.

Writing War Drama for the Screen

Writing a war drama for the screen means taking the emotional depth of your characters and the scale of war and translating both into powerful visual storytelling. It's not just about dialogue or monologues—it's about what the audience *sees* and *feels* without words. War on screen is movement, silence, sound, contrast, and rhythm. It's the moment a soldier closes his eyes before a charge, the way the wind moves through ruined buildings, the thunder of distant artillery, or a single tear tracking through the dirt on someone's face. Your job as a screenwriter is to make the viewer live through the war—not just watch it.

When writing for the screen, think in images first. Before you write dialogue, before you describe a location, imagine the shot. Picture the frame. Is it wide and desolate? Is it claustrophobic and handheld? Is it still and tense, or frantic and blurred? War is chaos, but on screen it has to be *controlled chaos*—with intention behind every scene. Use ChatGPT to help describe visuals. Try prompts like, "Describe a battle scene at dawn from a soldier's point of view in cinematic terms," or "Write a visual moment of silence after an explosion with emotional weight."

In war films and TV, dialogue often takes a backseat to action and reaction. What people *do* in the face of fear, loss, or duty says more than what they say. When you do use dialogue, keep it tight, purposeful, and grounded in subtext. Soldiers don't always talk about the war—they talk about home, food, jokes, nothing at all. But underneath, you can feel the fear, the stress, the sadness. Let ChatGPT help you write layered exchanges. Ask for, "A scene where two soldiers argue about coffee but are really processing the loss of a comrade."

One of the biggest advantages of screenwriting is using *visual storytelling devices* like weather, lighting, setting, and costume to communicate theme and tone. A war-torn town covered in snow feels very different from one drenched in summer heat. Mud changes everything. Rain creates silence. Fire is more than a light source—it's memory, destruction, cleansing. Use these visual layers as metaphors. A torn uniform tells a story. A limp flag in the wind can break hearts.

Action scenes, especially battles, need to be choreographed with purpose. You're not writing a list of gunfire and explosions—you're writing emotional progression through movement. A well-done action sequence builds tension, shifts perspective, and ends with a consequence. Whether someone survives, retreats, freezes, or dies, every beat of the action should drive the story forward or reveal something new about the character.

When writing these scenes with ChatGPT, be specific. Say, "Write a cinematic scene where a soldier loses his rifle during an ambush and must crawl through mud to retrieve it, while bullets fly overhead." You'll get something rich in texture that you can format into a screenplay. Or ask, "Write a dialogue-free scene where a medic works silently through the night tending to the wounded under dim lanterns," and you'll get an evocative piece that can be broken down into visual cues and screen direction.

Montage is another powerful tool in screenwriting for war drama. With montage, you can cover time, show emotional changes, or communicate how war spreads like a virus. You can use images to tell complex emotional stories without a single line of dialogue. Try using ChatGPT to help design these sequences by asking, "Create a montage of soldiers digging trenches over several days, showing how fatigue and tension grow." Then you can take those moments and layer them with music, lighting, or silence.

Also, remember the power of sound design. Gunshots and explosions are obvious, but what about *silence*? The ringing in a soldier's ears after a shell lands. The creaking of a bunk in the dead of night. The steady breathing of someone trying not to be seen. These are sounds that *build tension*. Use your script to note these cues when they matter. Write them in like you would describe a gesture or look. Film is a sensory medium—make your audience hear the war, not just see it.

Character development on screen often comes in quiet beats. A soldier staring at a photograph. A commander washing his hands in bloodied water. A child hiding in a closet, whispering a prayer. Let these small, cinematic moments carry the emotional arc. Use contrast—before and after a battle, before and after a loss—to show change. Don't tell us someone's broken. Show them walking away from a fight, not picking up a weapon, not saying goodbye.

The pacing of your script matters. War dramas need ebb and flow. Too much action becomes numbing. Too much dialogue loses momentum. Balance large set pieces with intimate scenes. Let the audience breathe—then take the breath away. Use ChatGPT to help you plan this rhythm. Ask, "Give me a sequence of scenes for a war drama that alternate between action and emotional introspection," and you'll get a structure that helps your story rise and fall naturally.

Lastly, the ending. Film is about what stays in the viewer's mind when the credits roll. A final glance. A gun left behind. A soldier walking home in silence. Write endings that *feel*—not just finish. War doesn't end with a line of dialogue. It ends with ghosts. Let ChatGPT help you shape a closing image. Try, "Write the final scene of a war film where the protagonist returns to the battlefield years later," or "Create a closing scene of a war drama that leaves the audience in reflective silence."

Screenwriting a war drama means wielding restraint and impact at the same time. It's about knowing when to explode and when to whisper. When to pull back and when to zoom in. When to write words and when to let silence say everything. With ChatGPT by your side, you can experiment with visuals, emotions, pacing, and tone until your war drama doesn't just tell a story—it *shows* it, *feels* it, *lives* it.

Because in film, war isn't only about conflict—it's about faces, shadows, glances, hands, footsteps, breath. It's about what stays long after the battle ends. That's the story worth telling. And it's the one that audiences will carry with them long after the screen fades to black.

Adapting War Drama for the Novel

Adapting a war drama for the novel means trading visuals and sound for language that speaks directly to the reader's imagination—and even more importantly, to their emotions. In a novel, you're no longer relying on cinematography, music, or actors to bring your story to life. Now, it's all about the words on the page. But that's also the power of the novel. It lets you explore interiority with intimacy, build tension across pages instead of frames, and create rich, layered emotional experiences that live inside the reader's head long after they've closed the book.

The most important shift in adapting your war drama from screen to novel is *perspective*. In film, you show. In a novel, you reveal. That means diving deeper into character thoughts, memories, and fears. You're not just describing what a character does during a battle—you're writing what they're thinking while doing it. What smells bring them back to childhood? What faces flash in their mind before they charge into enemy fire? What small thought keeps them grounded while everything around them burns? These are moments that novels do better than any other medium, and war drama gives you the emotional fuel to go there.

Start with your structure. If your screenplay followed a three-act structure or episodic format, you can use that as a guide. But don't feel trapped by it. Novels are more flexible. You can slow down and spend an entire chapter inside a soldier's head while he lies wounded in a field. You can jump perspectives between a resistance fighter, a civilian, a nurse, and a general, using each one to give a fuller picture of the war. The screen demands focus. The novel allows exploration.

When adapting battle scenes, you'll want to go beyond the choreography. Readers don't just want to know who shoots and who dies—they want to feel the *confusion*, the *fear*, the *surge of instinct*. Describe the sounds, the smells, the weight of the weapon in their hands. Use the rhythm of your sentences to reflect the pace of the scene—short, clipped sentences for chaos, longer ones for moments of suspended time. In a novel, the emotional *texture* of the scene is just as important as the action.

Dialogue changes too. In a screenplay, it's short, sharp, often visual in delivery. In a novel, you have more room for pauses, subtext, and thought tags. A line of dialogue in a war novel might be followed by a character's internal reaction, a flashback, or a subtle emotional observation. Let ChatGPT help you adapt dialogue-heavy scenes by expanding the internal responses. For example, prompt: "Expand this line of dialogue into a full scene with inner thoughts and sensory details: 'We'll never make it through the night.'"

One of the most powerful tools you gain in a novel is *narrative voice*. You can write in first-person for raw immediacy, third-person limited for deep focus, or omniscient to show the war unfolding on a larger scale. You can use flashbacks, letters, journal entries, and memory more fluidly than film ever could. This freedom lets you deepen your characters and themes in ways that are hard to capture on screen. You can also explore the contrast between what's happening in the war and what your characters are thinking, giving the story even more tension and emotional complexity.

Don't forget the value of *slowness*. In film, you often have to keep things moving. But novels can linger. A character can sit and polish their boots for three paragraphs, thinking about their dead brother. A nurse can wash blood from her hands while reliving a moment of failure. These aren't filler—they're the soul of the story. Use that space. Lean into it.

Also, remember that worldbuilding in novels is done through *accumulation*. You don't get to show a war-torn village in a single sweeping camera shot. You have to build it through sensory detail, through what characters notice, and how they respond. Let ChatGPT help with layered descriptions. Prompt it with: "Describe a destroyed church in a war zone from the perspective of a grieving soldier who lost faith," and you'll get material you can shape into something rich with symbolism and emotion.

A novel also gives you the ability to *expand themes*. If your screenplay hinted at the moral ambiguity of war, the novel can explore it in depth. Characters can wrestle with their choices over several chapters. You can use motifs—weather, letters, recurring dreams—to tie the emotional journey together. You can show how trauma echoes across time, how guilt reshapes relationships, and how love survives in moments no one else would notice.

When adapting from screen to page, don't just transcribe the script. Reimagine it. Ask yourself what the characters were feeling between the lines of dialogue. Think about the scenes you couldn't include in the screenplay for time or budget. Write them now. Expand the emotional beats, the backstories, the silences. Use prose to bring the inner world of the characters to life, and let that world drive the reader's experience.

If you have a completed screenplay, use ChatGPT to help you convert key scenes into narrative prose. Prompt it with: "Turn this scene into novel format with third-person limited narration from the protagonist's point of view," then paste the scene. You'll get a solid foundation to build from, adding your voice and nuance on top of the AI's draft.

And finally, understand what makes a war novel *work*. It's not the scale of the war. It's the intimacy of the people inside it. A war story that grips readers is one where the characters aren't just caught in history—they're *changed* by it. Their scars aren't just physical. Their choices aren't just tactical. They carry the emotional aftermath on every page. When you write that honestly, the novel becomes not just an adaptation—but a transformation.

You're not just telling the same story in a new format. You're offering the reader a way to *live inside it*. And that, in the world of war drama, is the deepest kind of storytelling there is.

Finding the Poetic in the Horrific

War is brutal. It tears bodies, families, cities, and entire cultures apart. But in the middle of all that horror, there are moments—fleeting, fragile, almost unexplainable—where something beautiful glows through the cracks. A glance. A quiet act of mercy. The way light cuts through smoke. These are the poetic beats that give your war drama its emotional complexity. They don't erase the horror—they give it contrast. And in that contrast, your story breathes.

Writing the poetic in the horrific isn't about softening the violence or romanticizing tragedy. It's about acknowledging that even in the worst moments of human experience, there's still humanity. It's the soldier who hums a lullaby while holding pressure on a wound. The girl who picks a flower from the rubble and tucks it behind her ear. The shared cigarette passed between enemies in a moment of hesitation. These moments don't diminish the brutality. They elevate the soul beneath it.

When writing war drama, your task isn't just to describe the trauma—it's to show how people *live* through it. And one of the ways they survive is by finding poetry in their surroundings. It might be in nature—a sunrise that keeps rising, indifferent to the carnage. It might be in ritual—lighting a candle, burying the dead with care, singing a song before going into battle. Or it might be in memory—holding onto a mental image of home, a voice, a scent. These are the threads that keep characters connected to who they are, or who they were, before war tried to strip it all away.

Poetry in war drama lives in the *details*. It's not grand or sweeping. It's quiet. Focused. Intimate. A cracked photograph found in a pocket. Rain washing blood from cobblestones. A character whispering someone's name even though no one is there to hear it. You don't have to make these moments elaborate. In fact, the simpler, the better. Let the weight of the scene come from what *isn't* said.

You can use ChatGPT to help craft these images. Ask for sensory descriptions like, "Describe a battlefield at dawn after the fighting has stopped, with a tone of quiet sadness and unexpected beauty," or "Write a moment where a dying soldier sees something beautiful and unexpected." These moments aren't about plot—they're about resonance. They anchor the emotion of your story in something physical, something the audience can feel, touch, or see in their mind.

One of the most powerful tools for finding the poetic in war is *contrast*. The sound of birdsong after shelling. A joke told in a morgue. A kiss in a bomb shelter. Contrast is what makes the horror real. Without those small bursts of humanity, the violence becomes noise. But with them, it becomes tragedy. And tragedy is what moves people. It's what makes them remember your story long after the pages are closed or the credits roll.

Think about how your characters process horror. Do they turn it into art—drawing sketches, writing poems, collecting objects? Do they try to beautify death to survive it—closing a fallen comrade's eyes, fixing their uniform, saying a prayer? These are coping mechanisms, but they're also deeply emotional story beats. They give readers insight into what your character believes, or *needs* to believe, to keep moving.

Don't be afraid to slow down during the horror. You don't need to rush to the next gunfight or explosion. Let the quiet aftermath settle. Describe the air, the debris, the way hands shake while doing something ordinary—lighting a match, peeling an orange, tying a bootlace. These moments carry more emotion than a thousand bullets. They invite the reader or viewer to *feel* the impact rather than just see it.

Symbolism is another way to weave poetry into the horror. A tree that keeps growing next to a mass grave. A broken mirror in an abandoned home. A book with pages missing, still read aloud by a soldier who memorized the lines. These symbols become emotional shorthand. They return, they change meaning, they gather weight with every repetition. You can work with ChatGPT to brainstorm these elements. Ask, "Give me symbolic images that represent survival in a war-torn setting," or "Suggest poetic motifs that could reappear throughout a war story."

Tone matters. When writing poetically about horror, avoid making it sentimental. It's not about making war beautiful—it's about showing that beauty *survives* war, often in unexpected ways. That's what makes it powerful. A character may not say anything profound, but the way they hold someone's hand, the way they look up at the stars, the way they smile through tears—these are the real moments of grace.

Also consider the role of memory. Many poetic moments come after the horror, as characters reflect. A character might remember the way someone laughed before dying. Or how the sky looked the night they fled. These recollections are tinted with pain, but they're also the only way the past stays alive. Use memory not just to explain what happened, but to show what was *felt*—and what was lost.

Poetry in war is rarely spoken aloud. It's not about big speeches. It's about what sits under the skin. It's about what characters *don't* say. The way they stand at attention for someone who's gone. The way they avoid a place that reminds them. The way they linger over a simple, warm meal after days of hunger. These are quiet elegies to everything the war tried to take. And they speak louder than any battlefield shout.

When you embrace these poetic moments, your war drama transcends the surface level of history, conflict, and politics. It becomes about life. About what it means to hold on when everything's burning down. And that's what readers and viewers come for—not just the battle, but the beating heart beneath it.

So let the horror be real. Let it cut deep. But let the poetry breathe through it. Let it shimmer like heat off the ruins. Let it drift like ash. Let it remind your audience, again and again, that even in the worst of it, there's still something left worth holding on to.

Visualizing Scenes through ChatGPT Prompts

One of the greatest strengths you gain when writing a war drama with ChatGPT is the ability to visualize scenes before you write them—clearly, emotionally, and cinematically. It's like having an on-demand storyboard artist who paints with words. Whether you're writing for the page or the screen, powerful visualization is key to making your war story come alive. And with the right prompts, ChatGPT can help you map out everything from large-scale battles to intimate emotional moments, giving you a vivid foundation to write from.

Scene visualization starts with intent. What do you want the audience to *feel* in this moment? Tension? Relief? Wonder? Grief? That emotion becomes your starting point. From there, you can craft prompts that focus ChatGPT's response around what matters most in the scene—whether it's the setting, the action, the mood, or the character's emotional state.

Let's say you're writing a night raid on a small village. You can ask ChatGPT:

"Describe a night raid during a war from the perspective of a young soldier, focusing on shadows, sound, and fear."

What you'll get isn't just description—it's *emotionally driven imagery*. You'll get flickers of moonlight on rooftops, the creak of wooden doors, the rapid breathing of the protagonist. You can take that scene and begin writing with a rich sense of place and emotional momentum, even before you've typed a word of dialogue.

For larger-scale moments, like the start of a major battle, your prompt should focus on scope and sensory overload. Try:

"Describe the first thirty seconds of a surprise attack at dawn on a foggy battlefield. Focus on chaos, confusion, and the visceral response of the soldiers."

This gives ChatGPT a frame to build around. You'll likely get snippets of sound—muffled gunfire, shouted orders, the sharp buzz of bullets—and images like boots slipping in mud or hands trembling on a rifle. These details give you building blocks to construct your scene in a way that feels grounded and immediate.

Visualization is also useful in emotionally quiet scenes. Think about the downtime between battles, the human pauses in your story. Prompt something like:

"Describe a scene where two soldiers sit under a collapsed bridge during a temporary ceasefire, watching smoke rise in the distance. Focus on stillness, exhaustion, and unspoken fear."

You'll get atmosphere—maybe wind moving through rubble, the distant sound of birds, or a subtle exchange of glances. These are the kinds of moments that deepen character and theme while giving your story contrast and breathing space.

You can also ask ChatGPT to help you shift tone within a scene. Let's say your protagonist is walking through the remains of a battlefield. Prompt the AI with:

"Describe a scene of a soldier walking through a field littered with bodies, shifting from numbness to emotional breakdown as they notice small details."

This kind of layered request will result in a progression—an emotional arc that starts with a flat affect and builds to something raw. Use what it gives you to sketch the beat-by-beat rhythm of the scene.

For character-centric visualization, ask for emotional specificity tied to action.

"Describe a soldier digging a foxhole while trying to suppress memories of a recent firefight. Use tension, physical movement, and emotional restraint."

Now your scene isn't just a character digging—it's a metaphor for internal conflict. You get a physical task tied to emotional stakes. That's screenwriting and novel-writing gold.

If you're looking to visualize scenes from multiple points of view, ChatGPT can help with that too. Ask:

"Write a single battle scene from the perspective of three different characters—a frontline soldier, a field medic, and a civilian hiding in a nearby building. Focus on how each person sees and experiences the same moment differently."

This technique helps you build richer, more complex sequences. It reminds you that war isn't one story—it's many, overlapping, contradictory ones. And visualizing a moment from different angles forces you to think more deeply about the narrative as a whole.

You can also use ChatGPT to visualize transitional moments—the things that connect your bigger plot points. Ask:

"Describe the early morning routine of a war refugee in a makeshift camp, focusing on repetition and subtle changes that show emotional wear."

Or:

"Write the scene of a soldier returning to the ruins of a city they once defended, using the landscape to mirror their inner change."

These moments may seem small, but they're essential. They carry emotional continuity. They're where your story lives when the bombs aren't falling.

If you're writing for the screen, you can also tailor prompts to mimic camera direction. Try:

"Give a cinematic description of a drone shot pulling up from a burning village to reveal the larger scale of destruction."

Or:

"Describe a close-up shot of a character's face as they realize they've been betrayed during a mission."

These image-driven prompts help you think visually, even before formatting a screenplay. They help you pre-visualize tone and rhythm, whether for the scene or the cut that follows.

Another trick is using sensory prompts. Ask for scenes built around a single dominant sense. For example:

"Write a scene set during an air raid, focusing only on what a child can hear while hiding in a basement."

Or:

"Describe a soldier experiencing shell shock in a field hospital, focusing only on touch and temperature."

This narrow focus creates an intense, immersive feeling that makes your writing more visceral and unique.

ChatGPT can also help you reverse-engineer scenes from an emotion. Say you want a scene that ends in hope, but starts in despair. Ask:

"Build a scene that opens with a soldier crying alone in a trench and ends with them watching the sunrise, feeling the smallest flicker of hope."

You'll get the emotional journey outlined for you, visualized through action and setting. This becomes a blueprint for your own version.

Ultimately, visualizing scenes with ChatGPT prompts is about writing with *intent*. It's not just about describing what happens—it's about creating experiences. With the right prompt, you can step into a scene, feel what your character feels, see what they see, and hear what they hear. You can walk into the smoke, stand in the mud, and hear the silence after the last bullet falls.

So before you write your next war scene, ask yourself: What do I want the audience to see? What do I want them to feel? Then shape your prompt around that. Let ChatGPT do the heavy lifting. Use the material it gives you as clay, and mold it into something personal, powerful, and alive. Because the clearer you see the scene in your mind, the more vividly your audience will feel it on the page.

Layering Themes like Duty, Honor, and Regret

War dramas often wear their themes on their sleeves—big, emotional ideas like duty, honor, courage, sacrifice. But the stories that stay with us, the ones that carve themselves into our memory, do more than just state these themes. They *layer* them. They let these ideals twist, clash, evolve, and sometimes unravel across the story. That's where the power lies—not in simply declaring what honor or duty means, but in showing how those meanings change in the hearts of your characters as the war grinds on.

When you start layering themes like duty, honor, and regret, you give your war drama emotional depth. You give your characters something to struggle with beyond bullets and bombs. These themes are not fixed—they're shaped by experience, perspective, and trauma. What feels like duty at the start of the war might feel like guilt by the end. What once looked like honor might come to feel like vanity, or even betrayal. And what begins as a righteous cause can slowly morph into something your protagonist isn't sure they believe in anymore.

Let's start with *duty*. It's a word used in every war, by every army. Duty to your country, your commander, your fellow soldier. But the emotional weight of duty shifts depending on who's carrying it. For one character, duty might be a badge of pride. For another, it might be a burden they never chose. Some characters are desperate to live up to it. Others are trying to escape it. The tension between those two can be one of the richest dynamics in your story. And the best way to explore it isn't by writing speeches about duty—it's by showing how it *compels* characters to act, especially when they don't want to.

Then there's *honor*. A concept that's glorified in uniforms and medals, but in war, it's often murkier than that. Is it honourable to follow a suicidal order? Is it honourable to disobey when you know you're saving lives? Is survival itself an act of honor when others didn't make it? You can write characters who believe fiercely in honor, and others who believe it's a lie told to young men before they're sent to die. Let those worldviews collide. Let your characters question each other, argue about what honor means, and change their definitions over time.

Regret is where things get personal. It's where your characters reckon with the gap between who they were and what the war made them do. Regret doesn't always arrive in big, dramatic moments. Sometimes it's in the silence after the fighting stops. In the dream that wakes someone at night. In the way someone avoids a name, a photograph, a memory. Regret is heavy, but it's also subtle. And when you let it simmer beneath your characters' decisions—when you show how they try to make amends, hide their guilt, or carry it like armor—you create emotional complexity that readers or viewers can't look away from.

The key to layering these themes is to avoid isolating them. Don't treat duty, honor, and regret as separate boxes. Let them *intertwine*. A character might believe they're acting out of duty but realize they're actually chasing honor. Another might take an honourable stand and regret it later. Or someone might follow orders out of loyalty and then struggle with whether it was truly honorable—or simply obedient. These emotional contradictions are where the real drama lives.

You can use ChatGPT to help you explore these overlaps. Ask, "Give me a scene where a soldier follows orders out of duty but begins to question if it was truly the right thing to do," or "Write a dialogue between two veterans debating whether what they did in the war was honorable." You'll get conflict, reflection, and subtext—great fuel for writing emotionally layered scenes.

Also consider how these themes evolve over time in your story. Early in the war, characters might talk about duty with pride. Halfway through, they might say it with exhaustion. By the end, they might not say it at all—they might just act, or choose not to. That progression tells its own story. Themes should move, bend, and sometimes break. They're not static. They live in the choices your characters make and the consequences they carry.

Don't forget to show how different characters experience these themes differently based on background, rank, culture, or age. A seasoned officer's view of honor might clash with a recruit's. A civilian fighting in a resistance might understand duty as something deeply personal, not tied to any flag or command. A nurse might feel honor in saving lives while others find it in taking them. These differences create natural conflict and conversation, helping you examine the themes from every angle.

Symbolism is also a great way to reinforce your themes without spelling them out. A medal buried in the dirt. A letter never sent. A uniform stripped of insignia. These objects carry emotional meaning that changes with the story. You can use them to quietly echo your themes as your characters evolve.

And let's not forget silence. Sometimes the most powerful expression of regret or lost honor is a moment when a character says nothing. When they look away. When they walk past a grave. When they can't answer a child's question about what happened. These moments don't need words because the theme is written in body language, in atmosphere, in the stillness between lines.

Layering themes also means knowing that not every question needs an answer. Sometimes, a war story ends without resolving whether what the characters did was right. Maybe they don't even know. Maybe that's the point. Let your story be a place where the reader or viewer is asked to reflect, not told what to think. That's the power of layered themes—they stay with people, not because they're neatly resolved, but because they linger.

Ultimately, war drama is about pressure. And pressure reveals character. The more your characters struggle with duty, honor, and regret, the more human they become. The more those themes bleed into each other, the more honest your story feels. So don't write about war as an event—write about it as a crucible. Let your characters step into the fire, and watch how their values burn, bend, and emerge transformed. That's where your story finds its soul.

Writing Dialogue with Military Precision

War drama dialogue isn't like everyday conversation. It's sharper. Tighter. More measured. In combat zones, people don't have the luxury of long monologues or poetic tangents. Words are weapons. Words are tools. Sometimes words are the only thing standing between life and death. When you're writing war drama, especially involving military personnel, your dialogue needs to reflect that reality—not just in tone, but in rhythm, vocabulary, hierarchy, and emotion.

Writing dialogue with military precision doesn't mean turning every line into jargon-filled technical chatter. In fact, the real art lies in *knowing when to be clipped and cold, and when to let humanity bleed through*. Military dialogue is about control under pressure. It's about speaking in layers—what's said and what's not. And it's about the unspoken rules that govern how people communicate within the chain of command and on the battlefield.

Let's begin with *brevity*. In the military, especially in combat, nobody has time to explain everything. Communication is functional. It's short. It's about conveying maximum information in minimum time. That means dialogue in combat scenes should feel *compressed*. "Contact left!" "Reloading!" "On your six!"—these aren't just realistic. They also carry rhythm and urgency. When characters speak like this, the pace of the scene tightens. Tension builds.

You can use ChatGPT to practice this style by prompting:

"Write a scene where a squad is ambushed and has to communicate in short, clipped, military dialogue while under fire."

You'll get a feel for the tempo, the urgency, and how tone changes under pressure. These scenes thrive on sound—the snap of orders, the panic in clipped commands, the tension in silence after a radio goes dead.

Now contrast that with how soldiers speak *off-duty*. Between missions, military dialogue shifts. It can be casual, crude, sarcastic, or strangely intimate. Gallows humor is common. So is banter that hides trauma. The contrast between a hard exterior and what's simmering underneath is where some of the richest dialogue happens. A soldier might crack jokes about a close call, but their eyes give away what they're not saying. Or a seasoned sergeant might give a speech that's more about *avoiding emotion* than expressing it.

Military personnel also speak in a hierarchy. A lieutenant doesn't talk to a private the way they talk to a colonel. There's structure and tone, even when it's subtle. Orders are often given without question. But tension can creep in when those orders start to contradict a character's morals or mission. Use dialogue to express this conflict without getting overly dramatic. A line like, "With all due respect, sir," can carry a world of restrained rebellion. ChatGPT can help you write these layered interactions. Try, "Write a dialogue where a lower-ranking soldier subtly challenges their commanding officer without directly disobeying."

Military vocabulary is another essential layer—but you don't want to overload your script or novel with acronyms and jargon that confuse readers. Use key terms *strategically*. Terms like "suppressive fire," "tango," "exfil," or "ROE" can anchor a scene in realism—but they should be balanced with context or explanation through behavior. If you have a character say, "Set up an L-shaped ambush," make sure the following action shows what that means, even if the reader doesn't know the term.

A great tool is to pair precise military dialogue with strong *subtext*. A soldier might say, "Copy that," but what they *mean* is, "I hate this plan." A medic might tell a wounded man, "You'll be fine," while making eye contact with another soldier to signal otherwise. Precision doesn't just mean correct terminology—it means saying only what's necessary and letting everything else ride beneath the surface.

You can also experiment with different tones depending on the context. Pre-battle briefings tend to be matter-of-fact, goal-oriented. Mid-battle dialogue is urgent, instinctual. Post-battle conversations might feel dazed, shell-shocked, or laced with survivor's guilt. Use ChatGPT to shape tone by asking for variations. Try, "Write three versions of the same line—one during a firefight, one during a tactical debrief, and one whispered during a moment of grief." You'll start to see how delivery transforms meaning.

Interpersonal dynamics also change how dialogue is delivered. Two soldiers who've fought together for years might speak in shorthand, finishing each other's sentences. A new recruit might overexplain out of insecurity. A hardened officer might reduce emotion to a single line: "We lost four. Move out." That brevity isn't lack of feeling—it's the result of carrying too much for too long.

When writing military dialogue, pay attention to *cadence*. Realistic dialogue isn't just what's said—it's *how* it's said. Use sentence fragments. Interruptions. Long pauses. In a tense radio call, for instance, a sentence might break:

"This is Viper One, I've got—hold, taking fire—enemy flanking from the—"

That rhythm captures panic better than any description could.

And sometimes, silence is the most precise line of all. In military culture, silence can mean acknowledgment. Grief. Respect. Obedience. Defiance. When a character chooses not to respond to an order, or takes a long beat before saying, "Yes, sir," it matters. Use those beats. Let them do the talking.

If you want to layer in emotional undertones, ask ChatGPT for help with specific emotional dynamics. Try, "Write a conversation between a squad leader and a soldier who froze during a firefight. Keep the tone professional but emotionally charged." The result can be a conversation that walks the line between discipline and compassion—two values always in tension during wartime.

And don't forget regional accents, slang, or speech patterns—just use them lightly. You want flavor, not confusion. A few well-chosen phrases can signal background or camaraderie without turning the dialogue into a guessing game. At the end of the day, military precision in dialogue isn't about being cold. It's about *intent*. It's about saying exactly what's needed—no more, no less. That's what makes it powerful. In war, words are rationed like water. Every line counts. Every pause means something. When you write with that mindset, your characters come alive—not just as soldiers, but as people surviving the impossible, one word at a time.

Writing a War Drama in a Single Day with AI

It might sound impossible at first—writing an emotionally complex, character-driven war drama in a single day. But with the right mindset, a clear roadmap, and the creative assistance of AI like ChatGPT, it's not only doable, it can be exhilarating. You're not just typing words; you're building an immersive world, guiding characters through moral firestorms, and exploring human truths—all in a focused burst of creative energy. This chapter is your blueprint for pulling it off.

First, forget perfection. The goal isn't to write the final draft of your war drama in one sitting. The goal is to build a full, compelling *first draft*—a story that breathes, bleeds, and moves. One that you can later revise and polish. When AI is your writing partner, speed doesn't mean sacrificing quality—it means trusting the process and letting the machine keep you moving when your energy dips or your ideas stall.

Start with the *ending*. This is the heart of your story. Where does it all lead? Is your protagonist alive, broken, triumphant, changed? What has the war taken from them? What have they discovered? By starting at the end, you give yourself a clear direction. You can prompt ChatGPT with something like, "Describe a final scene in a war drama where the protagonist returns to a home that no longer feels like home." You'll get emotionally-charged inspiration that sets the tone for everything else.

Next, build your character. One protagonist is all you need to center the story. Use ChatGPT to flesh them out fast. Ask, "Create a character profile for a disillusioned medic in a fictional European war, age 32, with a haunted past and a dry sense of humor." Within minutes, you'll have a personality, a backstory, and traits you can immediately start writing with.

From there, give yourself a loose structure. You can do this quickly using the classic three-act model:

Act One: Before the war changes everything.

Act Two: The heart of the conflict—emotionally, physically, morally.

Act Three: The aftermath and resolution.

Ask ChatGPT for a plot outline based on your main character and desired ending:

"Generate a three-act plot outline for a war drama about a medic who slowly loses faith in their mission but finds redemption after a traumatic final battle."

With that outline in hand, you've now got your emotional arc. The character has somewhere to go. Your story has legs.

Now it's time to write scenes—fast. One of the best strategies is to write in *cinematic beats*. Instead of tackling the whole story chronologically, jump to the key emotional moments. Ask for individual scene drafts like:

"Write a scene where the medic treats a wounded enemy soldier while his comrades argue about killing him."

"Write a dialogue between the protagonist and their commanding officer about whether the war is still worth fighting."

"Write a quiet moment of grief after the death of the medic's closest friend."

You don't need to build it in order. Just stack powerful moments. With ChatGPT, each scene draft gives you a foundation to tweak, polish, or rewrite in your voice.

As you move, keep the momentum going. Don't pause to research every weapon or historical nuance—use ChatGPT in real time to answer questions on the fly. Type, "What kind of gear would a battlefield medic carry in a trench war scenario?" or "How does battlefield triage work in a mobile unit?" and keep writing while it gives you fast, reliable information.

In scenes that feel flat, ask the AI to rework them with a new tone or angle. Try, "Rewrite this scene with more emotional tension and internal conflict," or "Make this dialogue feel more natural for a weary soldier under pressure." ChatGPT can refresh stale sections quickly, helping you maintain flow.

When you're stuck, lean on visual prompts. Ask for scene descriptions to spark your imagination:

"Describe a bombed-out cathedral where soldiers are hiding."

"Paint the scene of a night-time trench under moonlight and incoming fire."

These visuals will help you write cinematic prose, even if you're planning a novel.

And don't ignore pacing. If you feel your story is dragging or racing too fast, ChatGPT can help structure breathers. Ask for ideas like, "Give me a transition scene where the medic writes in his journal, reflecting on the people he's lost." These scenes add emotional texture and deepen character without slowing down the plot.

Within several hours, you'll find yourself sitting on a stack of raw scenes—maybe ten or fifteen—each one a puzzle piece in your larger narrative. Now it's time to assemble. Arrange them in a logical order. Look at the emotional flow: where does the tension rise? Where does it break? Where does it heal? You can ask for help with sequencing, like, "Arrange these ten war scenes into a natural emotional and story arc for a feature screenplay."

From that sequence, write transitions. Fill the gaps. Link scenes together with introspection, movement, and action. Don't worry if it feels rough—this is still your first draft. And with AI helping smooth the edges, it'll feel surprisingly complete.

Finally, wrap the story with a return to your ending. Revisit your opening scene, too. Consider how it mirrors or contrasts with your final moment. That symmetry brings a feeling of completion that elevates your draft.

By the end of your day, you won't just have an idea or a half-finished scene—you'll have a working draft of a war drama. One that moves, breathes, and holds emotional weight. One that was built with speed but doesn't feel rushed. Because when you write with AI, you're not alone. You've got a creative partner feeding you ideas, keeping you on track, and carrying the weight of the structure while you focus on the heart. Writing a war drama in a single day isn't a gimmick—it's a new way of working. One that uses technology to empower your storytelling, not replace it. And when the dust settles, and your first draft is done, you'll have something most writers don't even realize is possible: a powerful, complete war story that began as a spark—and found its fire in just one day.

Editing Your War Drama with ChatGPT

So you've written your war drama—your characters are raw and believable, your plot is tight and emotionally charged, your scenes pulse with energy. Now comes the part that transforms your story from good to unforgettable: editing. And when you bring ChatGPT into your editing process, you're not just polishing; you're collaborating with a second set of eyes that never gets tired, never misses a line, and always has a suggestion ready when you hit a wall.

Editing with ChatGPT is like sitting in the room with an endlessly patient writing partner. It's not just about fixing grammar or punctuation—it's about reworking dialogue, deepening emotional beats, tightening pacing, and clarifying character arcs. Whether you're writing a novel, a short story, or a screenplay, this phase is where your war drama finds its sharpest focus.

Start with the *big picture*. Before diving into the line edits, you want to know if your story *works*. Ask ChatGPT to analyze your full draft. You can say, "Here is my war drama story. Can you identify areas where the pacing feels off or where character motivation seems unclear?" You'll get objective feedback on what scenes drag, where the emotion doesn't land, or where the stakes feel too low. It's not always right, but it will point you to sections worth revisiting.

Once you have the broad strokes, work through scene by scene. Focus on clarity and impact. For each scene, you can ask, "Does this scene effectively move the story forward and develop character?" or "What emotional beats can be strengthened in this section?" ChatGPT will break it down for you—what's working, what feels flat, and what could be added or trimmed to make it more powerful.

When it comes to *dialogue*, ChatGPT is incredibly helpful. You can paste a scene and say, "Can you make this dialogue between the captain and the private feel more natural and emotionally tense?" Or "Make this conversation sound like two soldiers who know they might not survive the night, but don't want to say it out loud." You'll get revised dialogue that keeps the emotional undertone while tightening the language. If something feels too formal or too casual, ask for another pass. You can keep refining until it feels just right.

Another powerful way to edit with ChatGPT is to deepen character *consistency*. War stories are emotionally complex, and sometimes characters shift too quickly—or not enough. If you're unsure whether your protagonist's actions make sense in a key moment, ask, "Does this decision align with the arc I've built for this character?" You can even paste an earlier character description and have ChatGPT compare their behavior across scenes. It'll spot inconsistencies and suggest ways to better align character motivation with your plot.

Tone is a big part of any war drama. You want a consistent emotional texture—gritty, tense, intimate, or devastatingly quiet. Ask ChatGPT, "Does the tone of this chapter match the mood of the overall story?" or "Can you rewrite this scene to keep the tension building without losing emotional depth?" Whether you need to add dread, hope, suspense, or catharsis, ChatGPT can help shape the tone to match your vision.

For *scene transitions*, editing with AI can help smooth out the jumps between moments. War dramas often leap between chaos and stillness, life and death, action and reflection. You can ask, "Give me a transitional paragraph that links this battlefield scene with the next chapter in the field hospital, maintaining emotional continuity." It'll help you bridge scenes naturally, making your story flow rather than jolt.

You can also do emotion passes. This means combing through your story and focusing only on *one layer* of emotion at a time. For instance, ask ChatGPT to help you enhance the theme of regret. "Identify places in my story where the theme of regret is mentioned but could be expanded for deeper emotional impact." Then do the same for duty, for fear, for loyalty. This approach helps you sharpen your thematic threads one by one until they're tightly woven throughout.

Another editing method is to reverse-engineer key moments. Take the climax or final scene and ask ChatGPT, "Does this feel like an emotionally satisfying conclusion to the character arc?" If not, have it break down what's missing—did the character earn this moment? Did their choices build toward this payoff? Did the scene deliver on the emotional promises made earlier? Then go back and strengthen the moments that lead to it.

Don't underestimate the value of cutting. If a scene feels redundant or bloated, ask, "How can this scene be condensed without losing meaning?" or "Which lines or actions in this scene don't serve the story?" ChatGPT can trim the fat without sacrificing the flavor. You'll often find that less is more—especially in war stories where silence, suggestion, and subtlety carry more weight than exposition.

For line-level edits, paste a paragraph or scene and ask for a polish. Try, "Make this prose more vivid and emotionally impactful," or "Make this internal monologue sharper and more reflective of a soldier's trauma." Use the AI to test different writing styles, to inject rhythm, or to shift perspective. You can even say, "Rewrite this chapter in first-person present tense to see how it changes the emotional immediacy," and decide if the effect works better for your story.

And when your editing fatigue sets in—because it will—ChatGPT becomes your tireless assistant. It doesn't get bored rereading the same scene ten times. It doesn't lose enthusiasm for tweaking the tone of your medic's breakdown monologue. It's always ready with a new version, a rephrased line, or a more powerful way to show the emotion you're reaching for.

Editing isn't just about fixing mistakes—it's where you *refine the truth* of your story. It's where the war drama finds its quietest moments, its deepest wounds, and its clearest voice. With ChatGPT, you have a constant companion in that process. It helps you step outside your own mind, see your story from new angles, and keep your creative energy flowing even when your eyes are tired and your doubt is loud.

So don't think of AI editing as mechanical. Think of it as sculpting with extra hands. You've built the marble block. Now it's time to chisel. Time to uncover the shape inside. And with ChatGPT by your side, you'll do it faster, cleaner, and more boldly than ever before.

Creating Compelling Titles and Taglines

A great war drama needs a title that resonates before the first line is ever read or the first frame ever rolls. It's your story's handshake, its first impression, and in many cases, its emotional promise. A title should evoke a feeling, hint at the central conflict, or capture the spirit of your characters. It doesn't need to summarize your entire plot—but it *should* stick in the reader's or viewer's mind, like a whispered secret they want to hear more of. A tagline, meanwhile, is your story distilled into a single sentence—a callout that captures tone, theme, and intrigue in one breath. With the help of ChatGPT, crafting both can be not just easier, but also a surprisingly creative part of your process.

Let's start with the title. The best war drama titles are often simple but rich with meaning. Think of *Saving Private Ryan, The Thin Red Line, 1917, Paths of Glory, Come and See*. Each one offers a glimpse into the tone and focus of the story. A good war drama title often implies conflict, sacrifice, or reflection without needing to shout it. Sometimes it's a place (*Dunkirk*), a date (*May 1940*), a name (*Jarhead*), a phrase (*Fury*), or even something more symbolic (*Letters from Iwo Jima*).

When working with ChatGPT, start by prompting a batch of title ideas based on the core themes of your story. For example:

"Generate a list of potential titles for a war drama about a deserter returning home after the war, dealing with survivor's guilt and regret."

Or:

"Give me poetic or symbolic titles for a war drama that centers around a brother and sister fighting on opposite sides of a civil war."

You'll receive a range of ideas—some literal, some abstract. Use those suggestions as a springboard. Even if none are perfect, they often unlock the part of your brain that *knows* what the title should feel like, and ChatGPT gives you the momentum to chase it down.

Play with contrasts. A title like *Ashes and Honor* suggests the destruction of war but the persistence of virtue. *The Last Letter* brings emotion, finality, and personal tragedy. *Echoes in the Snow* could be about memory, isolation, and something left behind. The best titles often contain layers—they don't give away the whole story, but they *hint* at the story's emotional core.

You can also test ideas by prompting:

"Based on this story summary, which of these titles feels most emotionally powerful?"

ChatGPT can help you weigh resonance, thematic alignment, and originality.

Once you've brainstormed titles, move on to taglines. These are where tone and tension come together. A tagline is a promise to the audience—what kind of journey are they about to go on? It's your story's emotional fingerprint.

A tagline can ask a question:

What would you do to save a life you took?

It can set up a conflict:

One war. Two brothers. No way back.

It can offer a statement of theme:

In the darkest hours, the smallest acts of kindness echo forever.

Or it can deliver impact with sharp simplicity:

Fight to return. Return to fight.

He left a soldier. He came back a stranger.

Not all heroes go home.

Use ChatGPT to develop a dozen or more variations. Try:

"Generate ten emotionally resonant taglines for a war drama about a medic haunted by the people he couldn't save."

Or:

"Give me impactful taglines that match a gritty, realistic war film with themes of loyalty, survival, and sacrifice."

Once you have several options, test tone by asking ChatGPT, "Which of these taglines feels most aligned with a quiet, character-driven war drama?" or "Make these taglines feel more poetic and less action-heavy." Refine as you go, combining the AI's perspective with your creative instinct.

You can even reverse-engineer titles from your favorite taglines. If you come up with a killer tagline, you might find that the right title is hidden inside it. For example, a tagline like *"War doesn't end when the guns go silent"* might lead to a title like *The Silence After*, *No Peace Yet*, or *When the Guns Go Quiet*.

Think about how the title and tagline pair. A title like *Shadows of Glory* paired with *What did we really fight for?* tells the reader or viewer they're not just getting action—they're getting introspection, complexity, and emotional weight. The pairing should feel complete, like two pieces of the same story puzzle.

If your war drama takes a specific angle—a civilian story, a resistance movement, a spy thriller within a war setting—you can tailor your title and tagline to reflect that. Try, "Generate titles for a war drama from the perspective of a child hiding during a city siege," or "Taglines for a story where the protagonist is a nurse in a front-line hospital." The more specific your prompt, the more targeted and compelling the results.

At the end of the process, don't forget to run your top choices through a clarity check. Ask ChatGPT, "Does this title suggest the tone and theme of a serious war drama?" or "Could this title be confused with a romance or comedy?" You want to make sure your title and tagline set accurate expectations. That alignment helps your audience connect with the story right from the first impression.

A compelling title opens the door. A compelling tagline invites the audience inside. Together, they make your war drama impossible to ignore. And with ChatGPT at your side, you can generate, revise, and refine until those words feel inevitable—like they were always meant to carry your story.

Publishing and Marketing Your War Story

You've written your war drama, poured your heart into the characters, sculpted scenes of courage, fear, and survival, and shaped a story that resonates with the raw humanity of conflict. But now comes a whole new battlefield—publishing and marketing. Whether you've written a novel, a screenplay, or a short story, getting your work into the world and into the hands of readers, viewers, or producers requires strategy, persistence, and a bit of boldness. The good news is that with modern tools—including AI—you don't have to go it alone.

Let's start with publishing your war story as a novel. You have two main routes: traditional publishing or self-publishing. Both have advantages, and the right path depends on your goals. Traditional publishing involves submitting your manuscript to literary agents or publishers who then take care of editing, distribution, and marketing. The process is slower but offers access to bookstores, media coverage, and professional teams. If you go this route, you'll need a strong query letter and synopsis. You can use ChatGPT to help you craft both. Try, "Write a query letter for a war novel about a young medic haunted by the people he couldn't save," or "Summarize this manuscript in 200 emotionally resonant words." It's like having your own assistant who can revise and adapt your pitch until it shines.

Self-publishing gives you speed, control, and often a bigger cut of the profits. Platforms like Amazon Kindle Direct Publishing (KDP), Apple Books, and Draft2Digital make it easy to upload and distribute your book worldwide. If you go this route, invest in a professional cover, strong formatting, and editing—even if AI helps with the heavy lifting, you want human eyes to polish it up. You can even ask ChatGPT to help you format your back cover blurb or write different versions of the description based on tone. Try, "Write a compelling book description for a war novel that balances action with emotional depth."

If you've written a screenplay, you'll likely be targeting film festivals, competitions, or producers. Services like Coverfly, FilmFreeway, and The Black List can help you get your script into the right hands. Again, presentation matters. Make sure your logline is gripping and your synopsis is clean. Ask ChatGPT to refine it. Say, "Give me five strong loglines for a war drama screenplay about a father searching for his son across a battlefield." You can tweak until it hits the right emotional note.

Once your story is published or circulating, marketing becomes the mission. For novelists, building an online presence is essential. You don't need to become a social media star, but you do need to be findable and consistent. Create a simple website or author page. Share behind-the-scenes thoughts, character sketches, or historical research that inspired your story. Blog posts like "The Real History Behind My War Novel" or "How I Created the Protagonist of *Echoes in the Trenches*" give readers something deeper to connect with.

For screenwriters, your marketing may focus more on pitch decks, proof-of-concept trailers, or networking at events. Use ChatGPT to help you prepare. Ask, "Write a pitch paragraph for a war drama series set in an occupied city," or "Summarize the emotional arc of my main character in one powerful sentence." You'll have sharp, compelling language ready for any conversation, panel, or email pitch.

One of the smartest things you can do is position your war story for a specific audience. Is it for fans of *Band of Brothers*, *The Pacific*, or *All Quiet on the Western Front*? Is it more personal and poetic, like *The Things They Carried*? Knowing your audience helps you target marketing efforts more effectively. You can even ask ChatGPT to analyze your story and suggest comp titles: "What films or books are similar in tone and theme to this war story?" Use those insights in your ads, your website, and your pitch materials.

Email lists are still one of the best tools for authors. If you're self-publishing, start building one—even if it's small. Offer a free chapter or a related short story in exchange for an email sign-up. Keep your subscribers engaged with regular updates, bonus content, or personal notes about your writing process. You can use ChatGPT to write engaging, emotional emails that make your readers feel like part of your journey.

If you're advertising, keep it simple and emotionally driven. Run Facebook or Amazon ads targeting readers of historical fiction, military memoirs, or war dramas. Test taglines and cover images. Use ChatGPT to write variations of your ad copy: "Write three Facebook ads for a war novel focusing on emotional survival and brotherhood." You can then A/B test them to see which resonates best.

Don't forget the power of reviews. Ask early readers or fellow writers to review your work on Amazon, Goodreads, or wherever your story is sold. Reviews create credibility and help the algorithm push your story to new audiences. Use ChatGPT to politely craft review request emails or thank-you notes to readers.

Film writers should also explore pitching platforms, virtual pitch rooms, or connecting directly with independent filmmakers. If you can afford it, shoot a short film based on a scene from your screenplay. A five-minute clip showing the emotional weight of your war story can open more doors than a PDF ever could.

Whether you're publishing a book or marketing a script, remember this: the most powerful tool you have is the story itself. War dramas carry emotional gravity. They speak to sacrifice, loss, courage, and survival. That gives you an edge—because stories with weight get remembered. Stories with truth get passed on.

And now, with tools like ChatGPT, you can polish, publish, and promote your story with professional-level support at every stage. Whether you're reaching readers on Kindle or pitching producers on Zoom, you've got a creative assistant who never sleeps and always shows up with fresh ideas.

Your war story is done. Now it's time to launch it. Not into the fog of war—but into the hands of people who need to hear it. Let it march into the world with clarity, strength, and a message that lingers long after the final page or the last frame. Because war stories aren't just written. They're remembered.

Lessons from the Greatest War Films and Novels

If you want to write a war drama that lingers in people's minds long after the final page or last frame, then it helps to study the works that already do. The greatest war films and novels weren't just stories of battles and bravery. They were deep explorations of what war *does*—to the mind, to the soul, to families, to nations, and to the world. They weren't about explosions. They were about *reverberations*. And they all carry lessons for anyone who wants to tell a meaningful, emotionally charged war story.

Let's start with a classic—**All Quiet on the Western Front**. Whether you experienced it through Erich Maria Remarque's novel or one of its film adaptations, it's the benchmark for honest, anti-glorified depictions of war. The power of this story lies in its intimacy. We don't get a sweeping geopolitical overview—we get inside the head of a young soldier. Through Paul Bäumer's eyes, we experience the slow erosion of innocence, the brutal contrast between patriotism and disillusionment, and the crushing reality that war doesn't care about youth or dreams. The lesson here is simple: war is best told through *human experience*, not through statistics or speeches.

Then there's **Saving Private Ryan**, which redefined the modern war film. Its opening sequence is a masterclass in visual storytelling, placing the audience not in the role of observer, but participant. But what makes the story unforgettable isn't the action—it's the emotional question at its core: "What is one man's life worth?" The lesson here is about *stakes* and *theme*. Every character is carrying their own burden, and every death has meaning because it ties back to the story's central moral dilemma. If you want your audience to care about the outcome of a mission, make sure the *why* is painfully clear.

Band of Brothers teaches another vital lesson—*community and perspective*. Across ten episodes, we see war through the eyes of many characters, each with their own lens. One episode might focus on fear, another on leadership, another on the horror of discovery. What binds it all together is the brotherhood. The sense that each man is just one part of a fragile whole. For writers, this teaches the power of the *ensemble cast* and how to use multiple perspectives to enrich the emotional depth of the narrative.

The Things They Carried by Tim O'Brien offers a more fragmented, literary approach to war. It blurs the lines between fact and fiction, and focuses on memory, storytelling, and the invisible weight soldiers carry long after they leave the battlefield. What you learn here is that war is not just fought with guns—it's fought inside people's heads, in the stories they tell themselves to survive. The lesson is about *emotional truth*. Even when your story is fictional, your characters' feelings must be authentic. Readers can sense when something is real. That's what connects them.

Then there's **Apocalypse Now**, a film that dives headfirst into psychological war. Inspired by *Heart of Darkness*, it explores the insanity and spiritual collapse that can arise from prolonged conflict. The journey is literal and metaphorical—into the jungle and into the psyche. The lesson from this film is that sometimes, the most important battles happen *inside* the character. War strips away identity, morality, and sanity, and stories that explore those cracks reveal truths that go beyond bullets and blood.

Letters from Iwo Jima and **The Pianist** teach us about *perspective*. They shift the lens to voices we rarely hear—Japanese soldiers writing home in one, and a Jewish pianist hiding in plain sight in the other. Both humanize people who are often simplified in war stories. The lesson is to *look closer*. Who's usually left out of war narratives? Whose voice hasn't been heard? Tell that story, and you're already doing something powerful.

A more recent example is **1917**, which stands out because of its technical execution—designed to appear as one continuous shot. But beyond the cinematic trick, the film delivers a tightly-focused emotional journey. Two men. One mission. A relentless ticking clock. The lesson here is about *simplicity*. You don't need dozens of characters and subplots. Sometimes one character, one goal, and one day can be enough to break hearts and raise tension. Keep it focused, and let the intensity build naturally.

And then there's **Come and See**, a lesser-known but devastating Russian film. It doesn't just show war—it makes you feel as though you're living inside it. It's a descent into madness, shot with surreal horror and emotional realism. The lesson is about *immersion*. If you can bring your reader or viewer deep enough into your protagonist's world, the emotional weight will hit harder than any speech or explosion ever could.

Every great war story, whether on screen or in print, offers a variation of one key theme: **war changes people**. Sometimes it breaks them. Sometimes it builds them into something new. Sometimes it strips everything away until all that's left is one human, standing in silence, asking what it was all for. Your job as a war writer isn't to glorify or condemn—it's to *explore*. To walk with your characters through the mud, the fear, the hope, the trauma, and let the audience feel something real.

Use ChatGPT to help study these classics. Ask for thematic breakdowns. Say, "What are the central emotional arcs in *The Thin Red Line*?" or "What made *Saving Private Ryan* so effective at balancing action and emotion?" Let the AI help you dissect structure, character arcs, visual motifs, and tone. Use what works for your own story—but don't copy. Be inspired. Learn the rhythms, the choices, and then put your own voice into the next great war story.

Because the best war dramas—whether born from novels or films—aren't really about war. They're about people. About humanity under pressure. And that's a lesson worth remembering every time you sit down to write.

Why Your War Drama Matters Today

You might wonder, with all the stories already written about war—ancient conflicts, world wars, civil wars, modern-day battles—what more is there to say? Why write another war drama when the world already seems heavy with violence and chaos? But here's the truth: your war story matters *because* the world is still wrestling with conflict. Because war never truly ends—it just changes shape, shifts location, takes on new names. Your war drama can give voice to something we're still trying to understand: what it means to be human in the face of destruction.

Your story matters today because it's not just about guns and uniforms. It's about the people caught in the middle. The soldier. The medic. The child. The refugee. The deserter. The survivor. War stories put a human face on events that are often reduced to headlines or statistics. They pull us out of the abstract and into the emotional. They remind us that behind every conflict there are mothers, brothers, lovers, friends—ordinary people in extraordinary circumstances.

Writing a war drama today also gives you the chance to reflect the *current emotional landscape* of the world. Whether your story is historical, fictional, or futuristic, it speaks to something we're all feeling right now—fear, division, the hunger for peace, the longing for connection, and the questions we ask when violence seems endless. Your story doesn't have to be set in the modern era to comment on modern concerns. War stories have always been mirrors, and the best ones show us who we are—and who we could be.

Your war drama might be about duty, but underneath, it's about identity. It might be about combat, but underneath, it's about survival. It might be about betrayal, but underneath, it's about trust, loyalty, and heartbreak. These are themes that transcend time. And in a world where people are increasingly distanced from one another—politically, culturally, emotionally—your story has the power to rebuild empathy, one scene at a time.

Maybe your protagonist is a reluctant hero who doesn't believe in the fight, but fights anyway to protect someone they love. Maybe it's a story of resistance, where the battle isn't on the frontlines but in the quiet acts of defiance against oppression. Maybe it's about healing—the slow, painful work of rebuilding after the war is over. These stories matter because they ask us to feel. They ask us to understand. And more than anything, they ask us not to forget.

In a time when news cycles move fast and attention spans grow short, fiction—especially fiction grounded in truth—still has the power to make people *pause.* To think. To care. Your war drama, if told with honesty and depth, can cut through the noise. It can remind people of the cost of war—not in numbers, but in faces, voices, dreams lost and memories carried.

Technology gives you the tools to bring this story to life faster than ever before. With the help of ChatGPT, you can write vivid scenes, create complex characters, explore history, and develop emotionally rich dialogue—all in a day if you're driven enough. But the speed of creation doesn't cheapen the story. It frees you to focus on what really matters: the emotional truth.

Your war drama can speak for those who can't. It can carry the memory of real people who lived and died in war. It can challenge assumptions, expose injustice, and honor courage in its quietest forms. It can open doors for readers or viewers to see themselves in people from another time, another country, another side. And sometimes, that's enough to build a bridge where none existed before.

It can also offer healing. For readers who've lived through conflict. For families who've lost someone. For anyone trying to make sense of a world that often feels senseless. Your war story might be fiction, but its emotional resonance can be very real. Sometimes, a character's pain can say what a person hasn't been able to put into words. Sometimes, a fictional war can reveal something painfully true about the world we're living in.

And most importantly, your war drama matters because *no one else can tell it the way you can*. Your voice, your perspective, your emotional truth is unique. You bring your own questions, your own experiences, your own sense of justice, hope, anger, and heartbreak. That individuality gives your story power. It ensures that even in a sea of stories, yours will find someone who needs it.

So whether you're writing a gritty battlefield epic, a quiet domestic war story, a psychological descent into trauma, or a sweeping story of survival, don't underestimate its value. Don't doubt its relevance. Now more than ever, we need stories that remind us of what we lose when we fight—and what we find when we survive.

Your war drama doesn't just belong on the page or on the screen. It belongs in the world. Because someone out there is still living through the things you're writing about. And someone else is waiting to understand. Give them that chance. Let your story speak. Let it march forward.

Because your war drama isn't just another story. It's a testimony. And it matters—right now.

Examples of Prompts for War Story Design and Structure

One of the best ways to use AI to write a compelling war drama is to ask the *right* questions. Well-crafted prompts lead to rich, specific, and emotionally grounded content. Think of prompts as the blueprint to your story—they can help you develop characters, explore setting, build plot structure, and even fine-tune emotional arcs. When writing a war drama, your prompts should reflect the complexity of the world you're building, the tension of the battlefield, and the quiet devastation in the moments in between.

To design your war story from the ground up, start by working with foundational prompts that define the narrative's core elements—theme, setting, characters, and emotional trajectory.

Here are some of the best types of prompts you can use, categorized by purpose:

1. Character Creation and Development

Ask prompts that create layered, conflicted characters shaped by war. These should help you define backstory, emotional conflict, and personality:

- "Create a character profile for a former soldier who deserted during the war and now lives in hiding. Include internal conflicts and emotional trauma."
- "Describe a young nurse working on the frontlines who tries to stay hopeful but has lost faith in humanity."
- "Give me five morally complex protagonists for a war drama, each with a personal reason for joining the fight."

You can also shape their arcs with prompts like:

- "What is the emotional journey of a soldier who begins as idealistic but becomes disillusioned after a failed mission?"
- "Describe how a resistance fighter changes from vengeful to forgiving over the course of a war drama."

2. Conflict and Plot Structure

Strong prompts for plotting a war drama focus on moral tension, internal versus external conflict, and the irreversible effects of war:

- "Outline a three-act structure for a war story centered around a father searching for his son on the battlefield."
- "Create a plot outline for a war drama where a soldier begins to question his orders and ultimately turns against his commander."
- "Design a war story that takes place in a besieged city and follows civilians trying to escape over seven days."

To deepen plot complexity, try:

- "Suggest five major turning points in a war story where trust between characters is tested."
- "Give me a plot idea where a soldier's secret threatens the entire mission."

3. Setting and Atmosphere

War dramas are as much about atmosphere as they are about events. Use prompts to establish sensory detail, cultural depth, and emotional tone:

- "Describe a war-torn village in winter from the point of view of a soldier seeing it for the first time."
- "What would the mood be like in a bunker during a ceasefire after weeks of fighting?"
- "Generate a vivid description of a military hospital near the frontlines where chaos and compassion intersect."

You can also experiment with metaphorical settings:

- "Design a symbolic setting in a war story where nature is reclaiming the battlefield."

4. Dialogue and Emotional Tension

Good war drama dialogue is layered and loaded with subtext. Prompts can help you practice writing tension without exposition:

- "Write a conversation between two soldiers debating whether their commanding officer made the right call after a failed mission."
- "Write a scene where a medic quietly tends to an enemy soldier while ignoring the judgmental looks of comrades."
- "Create a tense dialogue where a character must admit they caused another's death—but can't say it directly."

5. Exploring Theme

Use prompts to design thematic elements that will thread through your story and carry emotional weight:

- "Explore the theme of regret in a war story by listing five scenes that gradually build to a character's confession."
- "Suggest ways to portray honor through both action and silence in a war drama."
- "Give me a symbolic motif for a war story built around the idea of memory and forgetting."

6. Experimental Structures and Narrative Style

You can use ChatGPT to explore unconventional formats or story delivery methods:

- "Outline a war story told entirely through letters between a mother and her son on the frontlines."
- "Give me a chapter breakdown for a war novel that switches between two soldiers on opposite sides of the same conflict."
- "Design a nonlinear war story that begins at the end of the war and moves backward toward its beginning."

7. Emotional Scene Building

For specific moments in your story, prompts can help flesh out scenes that land with emotional power:

- "Describe a moment when a soldier realizes they're the only one from their squad who survived an ambush."

- "Write a scene where a character stumbles upon a child in the ruins of a city and has to choose between staying hidden or helping."
- "Give me a moment of calm before a surprise attack that focuses on camaraderie and normalcy."

8. Internal Monologues and Voice

War is deeply internal. Use prompts to find your characters' voices and interior worlds:

- "Write an internal monologue of a war veteran attending a memorial years after the conflict, remembering those who didn't make it."
- "Describe the thoughts of a soldier who is about to go over the top, knowing it may be their last moment."
- "Give me a journal entry from a resistance fighter on the night before a dangerous mission."

9. Symbolism and Motifs

Symbolic elements can deepen your war drama's emotional texture:

- "Suggest symbolic objects that represent hope, grief, or survival in a war drama."
- "What recurring visual or natural element can be used to track a character's psychological decline in a war story?"

10. Worldbuilding for Fictional Wars

If you're designing a fictional war, prompts can help shape the history, politics, and cultures involved:

- "Create a brief history of a fictional war between two neighboring nations with religious and economic tensions."
- "Describe a fictional battlefield environment that has become uninhabitable due to years of conflict."
- "Design two opposing military forces with unique philosophies, strategies, and gear for a futuristic war drama."

The beauty of working with ChatGPT is that each of these prompts can evolve. You can build on one prompt's result with follow-ups like:

"Add more internal conflict,"

"Make it more cinematic,"

"Describe the scene from another character's point of view,"

or "Turn this into a climactic moment."

By prompting with clarity, emotion, and specificity, you're not just getting random ideas—you're building a full emotional and narrative framework, piece by piece. Whether you're drafting from scratch or refining an outline, these kinds of prompts help ensure that your war story has weight, rhythm, and heart. And in the end, that's what all great war dramas are made of.

Examples of Prompts for Designing Compelling Characters

Every unforgettable war story is built on the backs of unforgettable characters. Whether they're leading a charge into battle, burying the dead after the shelling stops, or writing a final letter home, these characters are the emotional core of your story. A war drama can have thrilling action, historical relevance, and stunning settings—but without compelling characters, none of it will stick. That's why designing your characters with powerful prompts is one of the most important things you can do when building a war narrative. And with ChatGPT, you have the perfect creative partner to help you dig deep and build characters that feel fully alive.

Good character prompts should go beyond simple descriptions. They should uncover *motivations, contradictions, trauma, desire, regret*, and *hope*. Your characters should feel like they've lived a life before the story begins—and like they'll carry the weight of what happens long after it ends.

Here are some of the best types of prompts to create emotionally rich and realistic characters for your war drama:

1. General Character Design

Start with prompts that help you flesh out a basic character profile, especially when you're looking to build out your core cast.

- "Create a compelling war drama protagonist who begins the story as idealistic but slowly becomes disillusioned."
- "Design a secondary character who acts tough but is secretly terrified of combat. Include their background, how they joined the war, and how they hide their fear."
- "Invent a war nurse who once trained as an artist and uses sketching as a coping mechanism. What is her emotional arc during the story?"

You can specify gender, nationality, age, beliefs, or experience levels in your prompt to tailor the outcome.

2. Character Archetypes with a Twist

Sometimes starting with an archetype and then flipping it leads to fascinating results. Try prompts like:

- "Give me five unique war drama characters based on classic archetypes (the hero, the coward, the commander, the innocent, the traitor) with emotional complexity and moral contradictions."
- "Create a pacifist trapped in a war zone who is forced to make violent decisions. What motivates them? How do they justify their actions?"
- "Design a war journalist who begins as an observer and slowly becomes a participant."

3. Emotional Conflicts and Internal Struggles

A character's internal world is often more important than their actions. Use prompts to explore the tension between who they are and who the war is turning them into.

- "Describe a soldier who is haunted by a decision they made during battle. What was the decision, and how does it affect their behavior going forward?"
- "Create a character who doesn't believe in the cause they're fighting for but stays because of a personal bond."

- "Give me a war refugee who carries guilt for surviving when others didn't. How does this guilt manifest in their relationships?"

4. Relationship-Based Prompts

War doesn't happen in isolation. Powerful dynamics between characters create the emotional glue of a story.

- "Describe two soldiers who were childhood friends, now on opposite sides of a civil war. What happens when they meet in battle?"
- "Create a mentor-mentee relationship between a grizzled veteran and a new recruit. How does their relationship evolve during the story?"
- "Write the backstory of a soldier who's trying to protect their younger sibling in a war zone. What sacrifices have they made, and what's their biggest fear?"

5. Psychological Profiles and Trauma

To create characters who feel real, explore their psychological reactions to conflict, violence, and loss.

- "Give me a psychological profile of a sniper who is starting to crack under the pressure. Include how they hide their unraveling mind from the rest of the unit."
- "Design a character suffering from survivor's guilt who refuses promotion and isolates themselves from their comrades."
- "Describe a soldier with PTSD who keeps a journal but never reads what they write. What are they avoiding?"

6. Past and Backstory

Your character's history informs every decision they make in the war.

- "Write the childhood and early adult life of a soldier who joined the war for revenge. What events shaped their sense of justice?"
- "Create a backstory for a commander who once deserted but was forced back into service under a new identity."
- "Describe the pre-war life of a civilian who now leads a resistance cell. What personal loss drives them?"

7. Belief Systems and Morality

What a character believes about the war—and about life—creates conflict, purpose, and decisions that move your story forward.

- "Create a religious character who believes the war is part of a divine test. How do they interpret violence and loss?"
- "Describe a morally gray character who profits from war but starts to question their actions after meeting a refugee child."
- "Invent a soldier who believes in the rules of war but witnesses their comrades committing atrocities. What do they do next?"

8. Voice and Personality

How your character *speaks*, moves, and thinks makes them real. Use prompts to explore tone and voice.

- "Write a short monologue by a sarcastic war medic who uses humor to cope with death."
- "Create a character whose quietness hides deep observation and intelligence. Describe how they interact with others in a high-stress moment."
- "Generate three different internal voices for characters reacting to the same traumatic event."

9. Motivation and Drive

Knowing what your character *wants*—and what they're willing to do to get it—keeps your story focused.

- "What does this character want more than anything, and what's standing in their way during the war?"
- "Describe a war hero who wants to escape recognition and live in peace. Why does that goal become impossible?"
- "Create a deserter whose only motivation is to get back to someone they love. What obstacles twist their journey?"

10. Death and Legacy

In war dramas, the question of who lives and who dies carries emotional gravity. Use prompts to explore how your character sees the end.

- "Write a journal entry by a soldier who knows they probably won't survive the next battle."
- "Design a character whose death changes the course of the protagonist's arc. Why did they matter?"
- "Create a funeral scene for a fallen comrade, showing how different characters react based on their personal relationship to the deceased."

Once you've generated character profiles and emotional outlines, use ChatGPT to drill down even further:

- "What keeps this character awake at night?"
- "What lie do they tell themselves?"
- "What would break them?"
- "What would redeem them?"

These aren't just prompts for data—they're prompts for *empathy*. For depth. For truth. When you design characters with this kind of detail, your war drama doesn't just show war—it lets us *feel* what it costs. And in a genre full of spectacle, that kind of emotional realism is what makes your story unforgettable.

Examples of World Building Prompts for War Stories

World-building in a war drama isn't just about maps, uniforms, or battlefield layouts. It's about atmosphere. It's about building a world that breathes conflict—where every location, culture, social norm, and political structure has been shaped, scarred, or shattered by war. Whether your story is grounded in historical reality, alternate history, or set in a fictional or future world, strong world-building turns your setting into a living force. It gives your characters context, your themes depth, and your audience something they can *feel*, not just imagine.

Crafting that kind of immersive world begins with asking the right questions—and using powerful prompts to draw out rich, textured answers. With ChatGPT, you can explore world-building piece by piece, from military hierarchy to the psychological landscape of a war-torn city.

Here are some of the best types of prompts to help you build a compelling and believable world for your war drama:

1. Historical War Setting Prompts

To write in real-world wars, use prompts to help reconstruct life, atmosphere, and ideology in that specific time and place:

- "Describe daily life for a civilian in London during the Blitz, focusing on emotional tone, surroundings, and survival rituals."
- "What were the unspoken rules and social norms among U.S. soldiers in the Vietnam War?"
- "Recreate the political climate of France during World War I and how it influenced attitudes toward conscription."

Use ChatGPT to simulate authentic language, class distinctions, and how war filtered into everyday life.

2. Fictional or Alternate History War Prompts

Creating an original war story world? These prompts will help generate deep lore, believable factions, and socio-political depth:

- "Invent two nations at war for twenty years. What were the causes, and how has the war changed both societies?"
- "Create the internal politics of a fictional military dictatorship fighting a rebellion. Include propaganda tactics and public dissent."
- "Design the history of a conflict between a nomadic mountain people and a coastal empire. What are the cultural values that fuel the fight?"

3. Environmental and Geographical World-Building Prompts

Environment shapes strategy, suffering, and survival. Explore how the physical world affects your characters:

- "Describe a war-torn desert city at the edge of collapse—include climate, architecture, and signs of past battles."
- "Design a jungle battleground where weather, wildlife, and disease are as dangerous as the enemy."
- "What would a battlefield look like if it's been fought over by four different armies in the same year?"

Use variations of prompts to build visual continuity and symbolic landscapes. War leaves marks—on the land, the buildings, and the people.

4. Military Culture and Infrastructure Prompts

Armies are their own societies. Use prompts to construct their belief systems, customs, and contradictions:

- "Create the hierarchy and discipline system in a fictional revolutionary militia made up of farmers and former prisoners."
- "Describe the training process for elite soldiers in a fascist regime—include physical, psychological, and ideological methods."
- "What rituals, superstitions, or personal traditions do soldiers in this army practice before going into battle?"

Also explore how the military interacts with civilians: Do they recruit? Intimidate? Protect? How does war shape civilian-military dynamics?

5. Civilians and Society during War Prompts

The world doesn't pause for war—it adapts, resists, and suffers. Ask prompts that expose what life looks like for everyone not on the frontlines:

- "Describe how food shortages affect the black market, daily meals, and relationships in a besieged city."
- "What are the social and psychological effects of living under occupation for five years?"
- "Create a fictional refugee camp at the edge of a neutral zone. What tensions exist between factions inside the camp?"

Use these to craft stories within your story—mini-narratives that give your world emotional weight.

6. Technology and Weaponry Prompts

Whether grounded in real-world history or set in a fictional war, use prompts to design the tools of battle:

- "Describe a new experimental weapon developed in secret by one side in a long war. How does it change battlefield tactics?"
- "Create the standard equipment and uniform for foot soldiers in a trench-based war set in an alternate 1940s."
- "Design the military vehicles used by two rival factions—how do they reflect each side's culture and strategy?"

You can ask follow-ups like, "What emotional impact does using this weapon have on the operator?" to keep the tech human-centered.

7. Symbolism and Cultural Mythology Prompts

War always exists within a cultural and symbolic framework. Build the mythology that makes your world feel lived-in:

- "What is the national anthem or war song of this fictional country? What do the lyrics say about the culture?"
- "Describe a religious or superstitious belief shared by soldiers about dying in battle."
- "What is the common symbol used in propaganda, and how has its meaning changed over time?"

These elements help you embed theme and emotion into your world-building.

8. Timeline and History Prompts

Create the broader historical background that shaped the current conflict:

- "Map out the last 100 years of tension between two nations and the key events that led to the current war."
- "Describe a peace treaty that was broken five years before your story begins—who broke it, and why?"
- "Give me five flashpoints in a long civil war that reshaped the country's identity."

This gives context to everything your characters experience. It also gives you powerful material for subtext, flashbacks, or world-weariness.

9. War's Aftermath and Post-War Society Prompts

If your story takes place after the fighting has ended—or is winding down—your world will still be haunted by the past:

- "Describe a city being rebuilt after a long siege—how do the people interact with the ruins?"
- "Create a society of veterans, deserters, and survivors trying to rebuild a broken nation. What new conflicts rise from the old wounds?"
- "How does a government rewrite history after a bitter victory? What statues are built, what stories are told?"

The aftermath of war is often just as dramatic and emotionally complex as the war itself.

10. Contrasting Perspectives Prompts

The same war can look very different depending on who's experiencing it. Use prompts to build conflicting views within the same world:

- "Describe how a soldier, a civilian, and a child each interpret the sound of a distant air raid."
- "Create a propaganda poster and then rewrite its message from the perspective of the opposing side."
- "How does a remote farming village far from the frontlines experience the war compared to a capital city under siege?"

Use contrasting perspectives to add depth, empathy, and realism to your setting.

Once you've generated your answers, go deeper. Use follow-up prompts like:

- "Add more cultural tension."
- "How does this world affect the characters psychologically?"
- "What changes when this same location is seen 10 years later?"

The goal is to make your war story world feel inevitable. Not just a backdrop, but a *force*. Something that shapes every decision, every emotion, every scar. With the right prompts and the right focus, your world won't just feel real—it will feel like history. And that's how powerful war stories are born.

Examples of Prompts for War Story Ideas

War stories begin with a spark—a moment, a situation, a moral dilemma, a relationship under pressure, or a single haunting image. That spark doesn't have to be loud or even violent. It can be a quiet truth, a question about humanity, or a glimpse of hope in the ashes. The goal is to take that spark and shape it into a full narrative—whether it's for a novel, a screenplay, or a short story. The right prompt can not only inspire a powerful concept but help you focus your storytelling lens on the emotional core of the drama.

Below is a collection of creative and thought-provoking prompts designed to generate compelling war story ideas. Whether you're writing historical fiction, speculative war fiction, or deeply personal war dramas, these prompts can open new doors in your imagination—and guide ChatGPT to help you flesh them out quickly and deeply.

1. Prompts Focused on Character-Driven Ideas

These prompts center around personal journeys that reveal the human cost of war.

- "A disillusioned soldier returns home to discover their younger sibling has joined the very army they escaped from."
- "A battlefield medic must choose between saving their enemy or their friend, knowing they can only reach one in time."
- "An orphaned child scavenging in a war-torn city stumbles upon an injured enemy soldier hiding in the ruins—and decides to help."
- "A veteran is sent on one last mission: to deliver letters written by soldiers who never made it home."
- "A young woman poses as a man to enlist and fight beside her brother, only to face unbearable choices when he is captured."

2. Prompts That Explore Moral Dilemmas and Psychological Conflict

War stories are most powerful when they explore the gray areas between right and wrong.

- "A soldier ordered to burn a village begins to question their allegiance—but refusing means death."
- "A captured spy agrees to betray their country in exchange for the safety of their family—but discovers the intel will cost innocent lives."
- "A general realizes the war can be won—but only by sacrificing a town of civilians. The decision is his alone."
- "A radio operator intercepts a signal that could save thousands—but revealing it would expose a secret affair with the enemy."
- "After years of fighting, a soldier finally gets a chance to kill the commander responsible for his family's death—but the man no longer remembers."

3. Prompts Built Around Unique Settings or Situations

Change the location, the rules, or the moment in history, and suddenly new kinds of stories emerge.

- "A submarine crew must navigate not only enemy waters but their own mistrust after a mysterious death onboard."
- "In the snowy wilderness between two borders, a downed pilot and an enemy soldier must survive together or

die alone."

- "A resistance group living in a city sewer system uses coded graffiti to communicate with citizens above ground."
- "During a ceasefire, two opposing sides are stuck in the same bombed-out hotel. They must coexist for three days—or risk reigniting the conflict."
- "The war ends overnight—but a forgotten unit in the jungle doesn't get the message for weeks. What happens when they finally learn the truth?"

4. Prompts That Use Time, Memory, and Flashback

These explore how war impacts the past, present, and future of those who survive it.

- "An old soldier begins writing memoirs but keeps omitting one name—until their grandchild asks the right question."
- "A woman discovers a hidden diary in her late grandfather's belongings detailing a forbidden love affair during the war."
- "Each year on the same day, an ex-sniper returns to a rooftop in the city he once occupied. No one knows why—until this year."
- "A young man finds out his missing uncle was a deserter and sets out to uncover why—and whether he's still alive."
- "A once-celebrated hero now lives in silence—until a documentary team comes to record his story and finds contradictions in his legend."

5. Prompts for Stories That Challenge Perspective

Challenge the usual framing by shifting the lens.

- "Tell the story of a war from the point of view of a gravedigger who buries soldiers from both sides."
- "A soldier begins questioning the cause they've fought for after spending time with an injured enemy prisoner."
- "A pacifist monk runs an underground hospital and finds themselves sheltering both wounded rebels and government troops."
- "A war widow becomes a voice of peace, but her public campaign threatens to expose a military cover-up involving her late spouse."
- "A military dog handler is separated from his unit and forced to rely on his dog to navigate enemy territory."

6. Prompts with Speculative or Future War Elements

Push boundaries by combining classic war themes with sci-fi, fantasy, or alternate history.

- "A war rages on Mars between two Earth nations, and the soldiers begin to wonder if they've been forgotten by both."
- "In a post-nuclear future, a former general now leads a small farming village—and must decide whether to rearm when conflict returns."
- "Two nations fight over the last freshwater source on the planet. A scientist caught between them holds the only key to peace."

- "A time traveler is sent back to prevent the assassination that triggered a global war—but the target isn't who they expect."
- "In a world where war is fought through simulations, a teenage gamer is recruited as a real-world tactician with deadly consequences."

7. Prompts Inspired by Real Historical Events

Sometimes the best ideas are based on real moments that demand fictional reinterpretation.

- "Write a fictional account of a soldier aboard the last boat out of Dunkirk, haunted by someone he couldn't save."
- "A group of Japanese-American soldiers in WWII fight for a country that placed their families in internment camps."
- "During the fall of Berlin, a nurse shelters both wounded Nazi soldiers and desperate civilians—including a hidden Jewish family."
- "A story set in the trenches of WWI where soldiers from opposing sides secretly communicate by passing notes through a tunnel."
- "After the Hiroshima bombing, a young girl wanders the ruins in search of her father, unaware he was part of the bombing crew."

8. Prompts That Focus on Legacy and Generational Trauma

The effects of war don't end with peace treaties—they echo into the future.

- "Three generations of a family have fought in the same war—and now the youngest wants nothing to do with it."
- "A soldier's child grows up in a post-war society that considers their parent a criminal—but the truth is more complicated."
- "A woman finds a trunk of wartime letters that reveal the grandmother she never knew had a double life as a spy."
- "A father with severe PTSD tries to raise a child who wants to enlist. The two go on a road trip to visit war memorials—and confront the past."
- "A filmmaker creates a documentary about a war his grandfather fought in, only to discover a secret that changes his family forever."

These prompts are designed to open doors into new and emotionally rich war stories. You can take any one of them and build out full characters, detailed settings, moral tension, and thematic depth with just a few follow-up questions. Use ChatGPT to expand them into outlines, develop dialogue, flesh out the world, and sharpen the story arc.

When in doubt, ask: "What does this character want?" "What does this war cost them?" "What emotional truth lies beneath this story?"

With those questions guiding you—and the right prompt to start from—you'll never run out of war stories worth telling.

Your One-Day War Story Writing Game Plan – From Start to Publish

Writing a powerful war story in a single day might sound like a challenge built for seasoned authors with weeks of preparation and caffeine on an IV drip. But with a clear game plan, a sharp emotional focus, and the help of ChatGPT, it's not only possible—it's creatively thrilling. Think of this one-day writing sprint as your very own mission. You're going to start with nothing, deploy with a fully loaded creative toolkit, and return with a completed, emotionally gripping draft that you can shape, refine, and publish.

Here's your complete, hour-by-hour game plan to write and publish your war story in one day—from raw idea to final product.

Hour 1: Lock In Your Concept and Core Emotion

Start with one emotional idea. This isn't about plot yet—it's about the emotional truth you want to explore. Is it regret? Loyalty? Courage? Loss? That emotion becomes your compass for the rest of the day.

Ask ChatGPT:

- "Give me five emotionally intense war story ideas centered around [insert emotion]."
- "Which of these ideas has the strongest potential for a complete story arc in a single day?"

Once you've chosen the idea, commit to it. No backtracking.

Hour 2: Create Your Main Character and Outline Their Arc

Build your protagonist. Keep it simple but emotionally rich. They don't need a detailed biography—they need drive, conflict, and something to lose.

Prompt ChatGPT:

- "Create a compelling war drama protagonist with a moral dilemma related to [insert idea]."
- "Outline this character's emotional arc in a three-act structure."

By the end of this hour, you know who your character is, what drives them, and how they change.

Hour 3: Build the World and Stakes

Now ground your character in a specific place and time. This doesn't have to be a real war. It can be fictional, futuristic, or alternate history—as long as the rules and tone are consistent.

Prompt:

- "Describe the setting for a war story set in [type of war, real or fictional]. Include sensory detail, atmosphere, and emotional tone."
- "Explain the stakes for the protagonist—what will happen if they fail?"

This sets the stage for your story to unfold in a believable, emotionally grounded world.

Hours 4–6: Write Your First Draft in Scene Beats

Don't write it in order—write it in *scenes*. Ask ChatGPT to help you develop emotionally rich scenes based on your outline:

- "Write a scene where the protagonist must choose between obeying an order or saving a friend."
- "Write a moment of quiet reflection after a brutal loss."
- "Write the climax scene where the protagonist finally faces the consequences of their decision."

Knock out 5–7 key scenes like this, each between 300 and 800 words. They don't need to be polished. Just get them out.

By the end of this writing block, you'll have the raw material for a full short story or screenplay draft.

Hours 7–8: Fill in the Gaps and Smooth Transitions

Now take those scenes and stitch them together. Add transitions, connect the emotional beats, and build the continuity. Ask ChatGPT:

- "Write a scene that links the escape moment to the final confrontation."
- "Add a transitional paragraph to show the passage of time between these two scenes."

By the end of this block, your story flows from beginning to end with emotional logic and structural cohesion.

Hours 9–10: Edit for Tone, Emotion, and Clarity

Run your full draft through ChatGPT in segments. Ask:

- "Make this prose more emotionally vivid."
- "Tighten this scene and remove redundant lines."
- "Polish this dialogue to feel more natural for a war setting."

You can also prompt:

- "Check this section for pacing and suggest improvements."
- "Does this character's arc resolve clearly by the end?"

Don't aim for perfection—aim for emotional clarity and clean flow.

Hour 11: Title, Tagline, and Cover (if applicable)

Ask ChatGPT:

- "Generate ten emotionally powerful titles for this war story."
- "Write a one-sentence tagline that captures the emotional core of this story."

If you're publishing it as an ebook, you can also ask:

- "Describe a cover image for this story—landscape format, no text, based on tone and theme."

Use that description to create or generate a simple AI cover.

Hour 12: Format and Publish

If you're publishing on Kindle, Draft2Digital, Wattpad, Medium, Substack, or even your own blog, it's time to prepare your final version. ChatGPT can help with:

- "Format this short story for Kindle using standard ebook formatting."
- "Create a short description for the publishing page that emphasizes theme and emotion."
- "Write an author note explaining what inspired this story."

Upload it, share it, and take a breath.

You've just written and published a war story in one day.

Post-Mission Debrief: What You Just Did

You worked fast, but with intention. You kept the story emotionally grounded. You didn't wait for inspiration—you summoned it. You trusted the process, used the right tools, and created something that didn't exist when the day began.

Now you have something real. Something with weight. And the next time someone tells you it takes months to write a great war story, you can tell them, *"Not always. Sometimes, it just takes one good day."*

I hope you found inspiration within these pages. If you liked this book, please leave a review where you bought it. Thank you from the author.

About the Author

Andrew Parry is a dedicated researcher and writer with a deep fascination for the paranormal, the unknown, and the metaphysical. His work delves into the mysteries that lie beyond the limits of conventional understanding, exploring everything from ghostly encounters and unexplained phenomena to theories of consciousness, time, and alternate dimensions.

Read more at https://lonetrail.blog.

www.ingramcontent.com/pod-product-compliance
Lightning Source LLC
LaVergne TN
LVHW082345200926
848481LV00012B/3456
* 9 7 9 8 2 3 1 9 7 5 6 2 4 *